Contents

KU-596-217

KEY TO MAPS

✈	Airport
🔆	Viewpoint
⭐	Start of walk/tour
ℹ	Information
203m	Mountain
A12 206	Road numbers

Introduction

During the Congress of Vienna, summoned in 1814 to resettle Europe after the Napoleonic Wars, attention turned to Italy where Napoleon had installed several members of his family as rulers. 'Italy,' said Prince Metternich, the Austrian statesman, 'is a geographical expression.' He meant that there was no such thing as an Italian state, even though there was an Italian language and an Italian culture.

Italian civilisation goes back at least 2,500 years, but during that vast stretch of time Italy has been a single nation only for the 400 years of the Roman Empire and for the period since Unification, which took place in 1870. For most of its history, the Italian peninsula has been divided into a number of small states.

This has been Italy's strength and her weakness. It was a weakness because of the endless bloody struggles that took place between these rival states, and because of their inability to combine against a common enemy. The first foreign invasion of modern Italy took place in 1494, and for the next 400 years the great European states – France, Spain and Austria – squabbled over it as they claimed this or that part of it for themselves.

But the fragmentation of Italy was a strength too, for out of this diversity came some of the dynamic tensions which helped to launch the great leap forward we know as the Renaissance.

Modern Italy is still a mosaic of small states under one umbrella and, as fast as you think you have found the final pattern, others pop up from underneath. Milan and Florence may share a common 'Italian' culture, but they are totally different from each other. Coming down to a smaller scale, Florence and Siena share a 'Tuscan' culture, but again there

THOMAS COOK'S TUSCANY

Thomas Cook first visited Italy in 1864 and took his travellers to Rome, Naples and Florence where they stayed at the New York Hotel. An improved rail service from Milan to Florence quickly increased the flow of tourist traffic to the Tuscan capital, and Cook, encouraged by this, opened an office in Via de'Tornabuoni. The wealth of art and architecture to be found in the city attracted many visitors, for whom Cook organised special art tours.

In the 20th century Thomas Cook became involved in the transportation of Florentine works of art through their shipping and freight subsidiary companies.

could scarcely be two more different cities. Coming down to a still smaller scale, Siena is divided into 17 *contrade*, or parishes; while recognising that they are all 'Sienese', each of these has a vigorous, independent life of its own.

These distinctions, together with the local loyalties they generate, are endlessly confusing for the foreign visitor, but they also add immeasurably to the country's cultural richness.

San Gimignano, a hilltop town with many tall towers

Introduction

Land and people

Tuscany provides a textbook example of the old maxim that 'history is a function of geography'; that is, people act in a certain way because of where they live. In the case of Tuscany, mountains have played a formative role. The Appennino (Apennine) range, under different names, curves around the north and east of Tuscany like a protective wall. The region therefore is a gateway between the north and south of Italy.

Coast and river

On the Tyrrhenian coast, Pisa controls the natural highway formed by the narrow strip of flat land sandwiched between the mountains and the sea. The road that runs down this coastal strip is still called the Via Aurelia, just as it was when the Romans built it nearly 2,000 years ago. Today, the main railway line also runs down this strip.

Over to the east, Florence performs a similar role to Pisa, controlling the passes through the Apennines. In 1944, Field Marshal Kesselring, leader of the retreating German troops, held up the militarily superior Allied forces by making skilful use of this fact, destroying all but one of the bridges of Florence in order to do so. Historically, Pisa paid the price for Florence's landlocked position: determined to acquire an outlet to the sea, Florence attacked its rival again and again until Pisa was finally conquered in 1406.

The rivers of Tuscany can be both a scourge and a boon, for, fed by heavy autumnal rains, they can rise in an alarmingly brief space of time. A vivid indication of the potential danger is provided in Florence and Pisa by the height of the embankments above the normal level of the river. Even this did not protect Florence when, in 1966, the embankments burst and the Arno flooded the city, causing immense damage and loss of life.

Rural life

Agriculture has, for centuries, been the mainstay of the region. The astonishingly fertile soil produces a great range of crops, including grapes, tomatoes, peppers and aubergines, while the upland pastures are used for grazing sheep that produce the region's famous cheeses. The Monti del Chianti (Chianti hills) provide Italy's best-known wines, and Tuscans claim, with justice, that their olive oil is the best in the world.

Until World War II, and even as late as the 1950s, farming methods had changed little, with oxen providing the main source of power, and much of the land farmed on the medieval *mezzadria* (share-cropping) system.

Mechanisation, reform of land-holding laws and European Union subsidies have since resulted in a rapid alteration of the traditional picture. Even so, many forms of wildlife still flourish; the wild boar (*cinghiale*) is so widespread as to be a pest to farmers – though providing sport for hunters and a favoured addition to the Tuscan menu.

Industry

The beauty of Tuscany's landscape and the splendour of its cities inevitably lead to the whole region being cast as an unspoiled rural idyll. This is by no means the case. Although its industries do not compare in size and variety with those of Lombardy, they are still an important factor. Tuscany is rich in mineral deposits, among them copper, zinc and alum. The world's largest and best marble quarries are worked round

Carrara. Livorno is one of the Mediterranean region's biggest container ports, and the whole Arno Valley, between Florence and Pisa, is lined with huge factories manufacturing glass, motorcycles and textiles.

The praiseworthy Tuscan determination to protect the core of its historic cities has not, unfortunately, spread to the countryside. Sprawling developments appear all over the region: little towns, like Greve in Chianti, are smothered in suburban development, and Florence now forms one almost continuous conurbation with Prato and Pistoia. Belatedly, a measure of protection is being extended to the countryside. Nature reserves (*Parco Naturale*) have been established in the mountains of the north, around the Garfagnana; in the south, on the Maremma near Grosseto; and inland, around Monte Amiata.

Land and people

Fertile plots in coastal Tuscany are used for growing tomatoes, peppers and aubergines

Tuscany

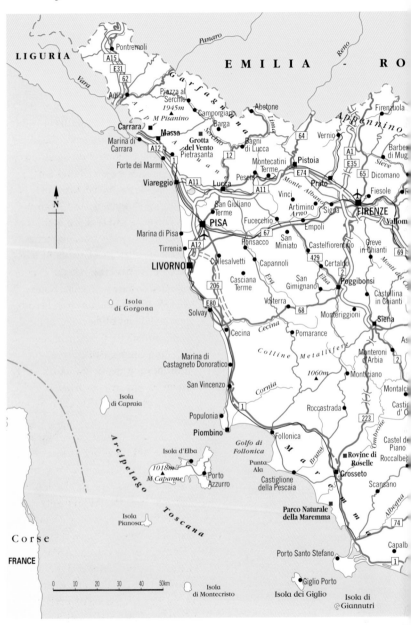

ITALIANS AND TUSCANS

The fundamental changes that have taken place in agriculture since the 1940s have deeply affected the people of Tuscany. One of the many Tuscan paradoxes is that these people, who created some of the world's most perfect cities, have retained their rural roots. Even today, in the heart of a city, you will come across some patch of vegetables, or a little vineyard, tended by a city clerk in the evenings. The great merchants and bankers of the past made their fortunes in the cities but always maintained a villa in the countryside – not as a holiday home but as part of an integrated lifestyle. Even the powerful and wealthy ruler of Florence, Cosimo de' Medici, prided himself on his ability to prune his own vines and till his fields.

City and countryside

At the heart of the Tuscan agricultural system was the *contadino*, the 'countryman', so-called because he lived and worked in the *contado*, the cultivated area that lay outside the city walls but which was regarded as part of the city, and which supplied the city with much of its food. The life of the *contadino* has been over-romanticised: despite the lush appearance of the Tuscan countryside, the work of a farmer can be brutally hard. Many of these *contadini* did not own the land they farmed. Instead they operated under the *mezzadria*, the so-called 'share-cropping' system which survived into the 1970s; under this scheme, the landowner took half of all the produce grown on this land as rent. The *mezzadro* had many faults, but it also ensured that the *contadino* had a direct stake in the land. Today, he is more likely to be an agricultural employee, financially better off, better housed (probably in one of the ever-expanding suburbs) but with no interest in the soil that he ploughs.

Incomers and tourism

Harsh farming conditions meant that many people abandoned farming as a way of life once the *mezzadria* system was abolished. This retreat from the land is most evident in the hundreds of villas which have been turned into hotels, and the thousands of farmhouses which have become second homes for wealthy urbanites from Florence, Siena, Rome and Milan. One entire locality has gained the slightly pejorative name of 'Chiantishire' because of the large number of British who have moved in (although, in reality, there are just as many Germans,

San Gimignano and the Tuscan countryside

Dutch, and even Americans, as British living here). Tourism, at first regarded as a lucrative alternative to backbreaking farm work or hand-to-mouth retailing, is now proving a problem because of the sheer number of visitors pouring into the region. The innate courtesy of the people who live in rural Tuscany, their amused interest in foreigners, means that human contact is still made, but with increasing difficulty.

An enigmatic people

Italians are perhaps the most self-contradictory people in the world. Passionately individualistic, they are also the people who have evolved the concept of 'the city' in its most perfect form, as a place where co-operation is the vital prerequisite. Their prolonged feuds and vendettas are legendary – a well-known proverb runs: 'Revenge is a dish best eaten cold.' At the same time they can be almost embarrassingly hospitable to a stranger. The Italians are the people who once elected 'La Cicciolina', a soft-porn actress, to parliament, yet they are also the people for whom the family is, quite literally, sacred.

They also invented the whole idea of machismo, but, as Italian journalist Luigi Barzini wrote in *The Italians,* his lighthearted but highly perspicacious survey of his fellow countrypeople: 'Men run the country – but women run men. Italy is in reality a crypto-matriarchy.' Do not expect to

The dawn light falls on Populonia's Etruscan tombs

understand Italians in a fortnight, or a year, or even a lifetime. It is doubtful if they understand themselves.

The Tuscans

What is true of Italians is even truer of Tuscans. They are a race of farmers and merchants, neither of them trades that are usually known for their concern with aesthetic values, yet they not only sponsored some of the world's most perfect art, they also triggered off the artistic revolution of the Renaissance which, in turn, profoundly influenced both the art and architecture of the rest of the Western world.

In a country where local patriotism counts far higher than national, Tuscans claim to have the deepest roots. They point out proudly that DNA tests show that they are indeed descended from the ancient Etruscans, and they seize on any characteristic which distinguishes them from the despised Romans – even claiming that Tuscan roads are interestingly winding while Roman roads are boringly straight.

Fellow Italians regard Tuscans with some wariness – the Florentines in particular, with their sharp tongues and even sharper business sense. They have the confidence of big-city dwellers, regard Florence as the best city on earth but treat the many visitors they receive with warmth and friendliness – if with a touch of condescension.

The Etruscans

The Etruscans remain one of the most enigmatic of ancient peoples. They dominated central Italy from around 900 BC until they were conquered by the Romans in the 3rd century BC. At the height of their power, Etruscan influence spread as far south as what is now Naples and as far north as Ravenna. We can see their tombs all over Tuscany, most notably in Chiusi, and the foundations of an entire city at Roselle, just outside Grosseto. There are at least 10,000 inscriptions in their language, written in a script which has affinities with Greek. We even know the names of some of their leaders: Lars Porsena, who led the attack on Horatius, defender of the last bridge to Rome, was a real person and King of Chiusi at the beginning of the 6th century BC. Legend has it that his tomb lies in a vast labyrinth somewhere beneath Chiusi. We know all this, but we still do not fully understand their language, nor do we know from whence

An Etruscan 'death house' in Populonia, Tuscany

they came; were they indigenous to Italy, or did they come as immigrants from the East?

One reason why we know so little is because their cities and many of their artefacts were made of wood and hence have not survived. Another is that the Romans deliberately suppressed and effaced Etruscan culture after the 3rd century BC. As a result, most of our knowledge about their lifestyle comes from their tombs and this has resulted in something of a one-sided picture, so that some writers have deduced that they were preoccupied with death. This is certainly not borne out by the exquisite wall paintings found in some of those tombs. The Etruscans were formidable warriors, as the Romans sometimes found to their cost, but they also seem to have enjoyed life to the full. The tomb paintings feature dancing lovers, young men playing the flute, and delicate country scenes. Most moving of all are the three-dimensional figures placed on their sarcophagi. Frequently these show a husband and wife, not grieving but seated as at a banquet, lovingly touching each other, smiling as they drink wine.

The Etruscans, though courageous and skilful, were ultimately crushed by the brutal military efficiency of Rome. The English writer D H Lawrence believed that they nevertheless triumphed in the end: 'Rome fell, and the Roman phenomenon with it. Italy today is far more Etruscan in its pulse than Roman, and will always be so.'

Rich frescoes adorn the interior of Santa Maria Novella, Florence

History

6th century BC The Etruscan federation of 12 states (the 'Dodecapolis') is founded: the members include modern Arezzo, Cortona, Chiusi, Fiesole and Volterra.

59 BC Florence is founded by Julius Caesar.

AD 476 The traditional date for the end of the Roman Empire after the death of Theodosius the Great.

774 Tuscany is ruled from Lucca by Frankish counts appointed by Charlemagne.

800 The Frankish king, Charlemagne, is crowned in Rome as the first Holy Roman Emperor.

978 The Badia in Florence is founded by the widow of Uberto, Margrave of Tuscany.

Around 1020 Guido d'Arezzo invents musical notation.

1063 Work begins on Pisa Cathedral.

1125 Florence conquers and destroys the nearby city of Fiesole.

1152 Work begins on Pisa's Baptistery.

1173 Work begins on Pisa's campanile (the 'Leaning Tower').

1265–1321 Dante Alighieri, author of *The Divine Comedy*.

1289 The Battle of Campaldino between Arezzo and Florence, the last time that citizen-soldiers take part; future battles are fought by mercenaries.

1294 Work begins on Santa Croce Church in Florence.

1296 Work begins on Florence Cathedral.

1299 Work begins on the Palazzo Vecchio in Florence.

1313–75 Giovanni Boccaccio. The introduction to his *Decameron* provides a vivid picture of the Black Death in Florence.

1334	Giotto begins building the campanile in Florence.
1342	Siena's Palazzo Pubblico is completed.
1348	The Black Death hits Tuscany: in Florence over half the population dies.
1377	John Hawkwood, English mercenary, made Captain General of Florence.
1384	Florence conquers Arezzo.
1403	Lorenzo Ghiberti commissioned to make bronze doors for the Baptistery in Florence.
1406	Florence conquers Pisa.
1434	Cosimo de' Medici returns from exile to begin a 30-year reign as unofficial ruler of Florence, a period of great artistic achievement.
1436	Brunelleschi completes the dome of Florence Cathedral.
1452–1519	Leonardo da Vinci, artist and inventor.
1458	Aeneas Piccolomini, the Sienese cardinal and humanist, is elected Pope Pius II.
1469	Lorenzo de' Medici rules Florence.
1475–1564	Michelangelo Buonarroti, one of the greatest Renaissance artists.
1492	Death of Lorenzo de' Medici, who is succeeded by his son, Piero.
1494	Charles VIII, King of France, invades Italy and enters Florence. Because of his failure to resist, Piero de' Medici is expelled from the city.

Statue of Dante at the Uffizi in Florence

1494–1512 Florence declares itself a republic under the leadership of Savonarola.

1498 Savonarola is executed for causing civil strife. Soderini takes over as leader of Florence, assisted by Machiavelli.

1513 The Florentine cardinal, Giovanni de' Medici, is elected Pope Leo X.

1523 Giulio de' Medici, cousin of Leo X, is elected Pope Clement VII.

1527 Rome is sacked by the forces of the Holy Roman Emperor, Charles V.

1529–30 Having patched up their differences, the emperor Charles V and the Medici Pope Clement VII combine forces to besiege republican Florence. Florence finally surrenders; Alessandro de' Medici is crowned the first Duke of Florence.

1537 Alessandro de' Medici is assassinated. Cosimo I is elected Duke of Florence.

1557 Cosimo I defeats Siena after long, bitter siege.

Florence rules most of Tuscany.

1564–1642 Galileo Galilei, the father of modern empirical science.

1570 The title of Grand Duke of Tuscany is bestowed on Cosimo I.

1737 Death of Gian Gastone, last male of the Medici line.

1743 Death of Anna Maria Luisa de' Medici, last of the Medici: she bequeaths all Medici property to the city of Florence.

1865–70 Florence is briefly capital of Italy.

1870 The Unification of Italy: Rome becomes the capital.

1940 Italy enters World War II.

1944 Retreating German forces blow up all the Florence bridges, except the Ponte Vecchio.

1946 Italy becomes a republic.

1957 Italy enters the European Community as a founder member.

1966	The Arno floods Florence, destroying many works of art.
1993	Referendum votes to reform government. Proportional representation abolished. A terrorist bomb damages part of the Uffizi and nearly 40 works.
1996	Florence hosts G7 economic summit.
2000	Millions of pilgrims pour into Rome for the Roman Catholic Church's Jubilee.
2001	The centre-right coalition led by multi-billionaire media-magnate Silvio Berlusconi wins control of the government.
2005	Pope John Paul II dies and is succeeded by Pope Benedict XVI. Berlusconi is acquitted of false accounting charges made in relation to allegations of illegal party financing.
2006	Romano Prodi takes office as Italian Prime Minister after defeating Silvio Berlusconi.
2009	Italy scheduled to take over Presidency of the G8.

Florence's famous Ponte Vecchio was the only Florentine bridge to escape destruction during 1944

Politics

In September 1992 a wave of general strikes swept over the whole of Italy, their sole purpose being to protest at recent heavy government cuts in social services. In Florence, crowds estimated at more than 100,000 gathered and marched through the streets. They were entirely good-humoured, with clowns, stilt walkers and children among their number, but they were also very determined.

Italian Communism

Displayed among the red banners of the marchers was the hammer and sickle of the Communist Party. Even after the former Soviet Union abandoned Communism, it survived in Tuscany. Italian Communism, admittedly, has always been a rather special form, and one which neither Lenin nor Stalin would have recognised. It is entirely possible for a Tuscan to claim to be both a good Catholic and a good Communist, simply adding to the confusion of Italian politics when viewed from outside.

An Italian word which foreign visitors to Italy would do well to recognise is *sciopero* (pronounced 'shioppero') meaning 'strike'. Whereas in many countries strikes are associated with poor industrial relations, in Italy the strike is also a strong political weapon, frequently used to put pressure on the central government in Rome. In order to achieve maximum effect with minimal financial loss to the strikers themselves, a disruptive system of sporadic strikes has evolved; various industries take it in turns to strike between, say, 9am and noon, or 3pm and 5pm, or whatever is appropriate. Very little warning is given to the public and one can never be certain whether, for example, a public transport strike will affect both the trains and the buses or just one of these. All the visitor can do is be prepared.

Antipathy to Rome

A common factor uniting Tuscans of all classes and political views is a dislike and suspicion of Rome, whose bureaucracy is regarded as a quicksand sucking in Italy's wealth. In Florence resentment was caused by a central government decree imposing an entrance charge on visitors to the Boboli Gardens. This seemingly minor issue aroused great local indignation because the gardens are one of the few green spaces in the centre of the city,

Politics

and are much used by mothers with small children. On a wider scale the decree was viewed as a typical example of Rome's interference in local affairs.

Another cause of dissatisfaction is the fact that the central government is responsible for the maintenance of most of the major historic monuments in Florence and Tuscany. There is widespread criticism of the fact that restoration work can trail on for years, with a harmful effect on the local tourist industry.

Historic divisions

This dislike of Rome is a reminder that Italy's political unity is increasingly under strain. Unification dates back to 1870, when the kingdom of Italy was created under Vittorio Emanuele II. The monarchy was abolished in 1946 and a republic created. During the winter of 1992–3 the disclosure of

Fountain sculpture in the Boboli Gardens, Florence

widespread corruption at the highest political levels created a wave of indignation throughout Italy. This culminated in a general referendum on 18 April 1993 when Italians voted overwhelmingly for a fundamental change in government, abolishing proportional representation which had contributed to the proliferation of parties, one of the causes of corruption.

Tuscany is one of Italy's 20 regions, and is in turn divided into ten provinces, each named after its capital city: Florence (which is also the regional capital), Arezzo, Grosseto, Livorno, Lucca, Massa-Carrara, Pisa, Pistoia, Prato and Siena.

The development of the European Union has given considerable impetus to those political movements that would like to see the north of Italy separated from the poorer south. One includes the Lega Nord, or Northern League, that advocates the formation of an independent central European state called Padania. Padania, as the argument goes, could become one of the most dynamic regions in Europe if freed from the bureaucracy and corruption of Rome. Though the right-wing Northern League enjoys considerable success in the north and represents a part of the majority coalition, most Italians are happy to live in a united Republic. Tuscans, true to their heritage as part of the 'red belt' of Italy, in general continue to favour centre-left party coalitions and dismiss the separatist views of the Lega Nord as extreme.

Festivals and events

Siena's Palio (see pp148–9) is so spectacular that it has overshadowed all other Tuscan festivals. Virtually every city has similar festivities, however, usually associated with a saint's day or with ancient rivalry between different parts of the city, and a distinctive feature of most of these festivals is that local participants dress the part, wearing splendid period costume. The following is a selection of the most important festivals. Since the dates can vary, check with local tourist offices for further information.

Viareggio Carnival

One of Italy's biggest, spread over nearly three weeks in February. Colourful boats ply the waters and floats are paraded every Sunday.

Explosion of the Cart (Scopio del Carro), Florence

At noon on Easter Sunday a dove descends on a wire from the high altar of the cathedral and ignites a cart full of fireworks. The ceremony is supposed to commemorate the First Crusade, when Crusaders brought back flints from the Holy Sepulchre in Jerusalem.

Exposition of the Virgin's Girdle, Prato

This precious relic is displayed to the faithful from Donatello's pulpit in the façade of the cathedral on Easter Sunday, 1 May, 15 August, 8 September and Christmas Day. On the Festa di San Stefano, which is held on 26 December, Prato celebrates the feast of its patron saint, St Stephen.

Game of the Bridge (Gioco del Ponte), Pisa

This game, held on the 3rd Sunday in June, involves two groups representing the two halves of the city. One on each side of the River Arno, they battle for possession of the Ponte di Mezzo, Pisa's main bridge. They do this by trying to push a heavy cart, weighing 7 tonnes and sliding on rails, over to the opposing side.

Feast of San Giovanni Battista, Florence

On 24 June, local residents in medieval costume parade the Florence streets, before teams from the city's four historic quarters battle it out in a sporting event. This used to be in the form of the *calcio storico* – a historical sport that is a cross between football, rugby and wrestling. However, in 2007 it was decided this was too violent and it has now been replaced with a boat race. The day ends with a massive firework display at 10pm from the Piazzale Michelangelo.

Feast of San Paolino, Lucca

A torchlight parade in period costume is held on 12 July in honour of the city's patron saint. A crossbow contest is held in the evening.

Palio, Siena

July and August. *See pp148–9.*

Joust of the Bear (Giostro dell'Orso), Pistoia

This contest takes place on 25 July when 12 riders gallop with a lance and attempt to spear two targets.

Bravio delle Botte, Montepulciano

The barrel-rolling contest takes place on the last Sunday in August between the eight *contrade* (neighbourhoods) of Montepulciano.

Joust of the Saracen (Giostra del Saracino), Arezzo

This medieval-style joust begins with a colourful parade in period costume. Then eight horsemen, representing the old districts of the city, gallop at a swivel-mounted dummy called *il Saracino* (the Saracen); the aim is to strike the centre of his shield while avoiding a blow from his whip. The winning district is awarded a silver lance. Traditionally held the first Sunday in September but with repeat performances in summer.

Feast of Santa Croce, Lucca

A torchlight procession takes place on 13 September in honour of one of the most revered relics of the Middle Ages, the *Volto Santo* (Holy Face), kept in the cathedral (*see p94*). A fair is held on the following day.

Crossbow Contest, Sansepolcro

This contest, held in September, originated in a dispute between the crossbowmen of Sansepolcro (in Tuscany) and those of Gubbio (in Umbria) over which town had the better marksmen.

Feast of the Immaculate Conception, Bagni di Lucca

This is celebrated on 8 December by a fair in the Fornoli quarter.

Burning of the Tree, Camporgiano, near Lucca

On Christmas Eve an immense bonfire is made with evergreen branches, announced by the bell of San Giacomo.

Period costumes mark almost all festivities

Impressions

'The traveller who has gone to Italy to study the tactile values of Giotto or the corruption of the Papacy may return remembering nothing but the blue sky and the men and women who live under it.'

E M FORSTER

A Room with a View, 1908

Tourist offices

On arriving in a Tuscan city for the first time, your first port of call should be the local tourist office (the addresses and telephone numbers of the major offices in Tuscany are given in the Practical Guide, *see pp188–9*). Tourist office staff are usually efficient and courteous, and most have a working knowledge of French, German and English. They will provide free maps as well as a range of well-produced leaflets, which are either free or sold for a nominal sum.

The siesta

One matter in which the Italians have entirely declined to accommodate visitors is that of opening (or, to be more precise, closing) hours. Everything shuts for three hours in the middle of the day and some sights are only open in the mornings. Shops, tourist offices and museums all put up their shutters 1–4pm, although department stores, supermarkets and some shops in tourist areas may remain open throughout the day. There is also a growing tendency for the more important museums and galleries to keep continuous hours.

There is only one infallible rule in response to this situation: when in Rome, do as the Romans do – and the Florentines in Florence and the Pisans in Pisa and, in short, Italians everywhere in Italy. Your options are to put off lunch for as long as possible, then find a comfortable *trattoria* in which to while away the afternoon hours (restaurants are one of the few types of establishment which do not close); take a picnic to some green and shady spot; or you can just go back to your hotel for an unabashed siesta. The world will come back to life again about 5pm and you will, by then, be more than refreshed enough to enjoy it.

Cash desks

Fiddling the books to cheat the tax man is a universal Italian custom, and to combat it almost every transaction is supposed to be accompanied by an official receipt. Thus, in the larger city bars, unless you are seated at a table, you must first go to the cash desk *(cassa)* and give your order. On paying you will be given a receipt *(scontrino)* and this you present to the bartender who will then serve you (in busy bars you will get better service if you put down some coins with your receipt!). To encourage compliance, an earlier law held both buyers and sellers responsible for making sure a receipt was issued. While buyers are no longer fined if they don't take a receipt, shopkeepers still might chase after you if you leave without your *scontrino*. Another form of cheating – buying fake merchandise – can be quite expensive for the consumer, who risks fines of up to €10,000.

Bus tickets

Another variation on the 'pay before you use' system is the obligation to obtain your ticket before you board a bus. There are no conductors and the driver's job is simply to drive; this is a good idea in terms of road safety, but presents problems for the unwary. Tickets are obtainable from most tobacconists, newsstands and bars (they are also available from machines at major bus stops in cities such as Florence).

Buy multiple tickets or all-day passes, since nothing is more infuriating than to find yourself without a ticket in a remote part of the city after all the bars and newsstands have closed for the day. Once on the bus you must 'cancel' the ticket by inserting it in a machine either at the front or back of the bus which will stamp it with the date and time. If you are caught without a ticket, you will be fined 50 times the fare, and no excuses are accepted.

Tickets last for one hour from the time they are stamped, allowing you to change buses. In Florence, three-hour, 24-hour and multi-day tickets are available, as are tickets valid for four separate 60-minute journeys.

Language

The Italians are an extremely tactile people who use vigorous body language to back up their verbal language and frequently touch the person to whom they are speaking. Do not take offence at this. On the other hand, be wary of that minority of males who still act the Latin lover, pursuing females with or without invitation. Italian women have long since learned to deal with this nuisance with a torrent of contemptuous abuse, a tactic not open

Florence is truly a painter's paradise

to most foreign visitors. The only real defence tactic to these amorous advances is to ignore them completely.

Outside the big cities and tourist centres, fewer people speak a foreign language. They are, however, delighted if you make even halting attempts to speak Italian. Tuscany is acknowledged as having the purest form of the language. Italian grammar is complex but many people find the pronunciation easier than other European languages. Many Tuscans pronounce 'c' as 'h' so that *seconda* becomes *sehonda*. With a few exceptions, however, each word is pronounced exactly as it is spelt, with the stress usually on the penultimate vowel (*see* Practical Guide, *pp182–3*).

City life

Florence is the only really big city in Tuscany, with a population of just over 380,000. Livorno comes a long way after, with a population of 180,000: then Prato (165,000), Pisa (105,000), and finally Arezzo, Lucca and Pistoia (90,000 each). All the rest are delightfully small and intimate: for instance, you can walk across the entire width of Siena in under half an hour.

Italian town planning has ensured that the historic centres of all cities – the areas of interest to most tourists – are largely untouched, although the surrounding suburban sprawl can be rather horrible. Even in a city the size of Florence, you can simply step out of the train or bus and start wandering

about in the city centre as though it were a small town. There's little nightlife in any of the cities – except Florence, Pisa and the seaside towns – but most people find it enough to sit at a pavement café in one of the incomparable squares and watch the world go by. That, after all, is what the Italians like doing best.

Country life

Tuscany is blessed equally with some of the most beautiful cities in Italy, and the most beautiful landscapes in the world. Even in a city as big as Florence you can get into open countryside within ten minutes or so by bus. Maps are not very accurate, and footpaths are rarely signposted, so don't casually undertake cross-country walking. However, following the lanes is a delight, while the mountains to the north provide spectacular vistas and, in most parts, quite easy walking.

It is possible to walk the width of Siena in less than half an hour

Campanilismo

For more than 1,500 years, from the fall of the Roman Empire until 1870, Italy had no central government. Region fought against region, city against city. The only safety lay behind the walls of your own city or *comune*. Crammed behind those walls, the citizens were forced to live together, developing urban skills, lavishing their best on the public buildings of the *comune*. A medieval lawyer said: 'Man is born first to God and then to the *comune*: he who hurts the *comune* hurts God.' Traitors to the *comune* suffered an appalling death – they were buried alive, upside down.

The great symbol of the *comune* was the campanile, the bell tower. Here hung the great bell which was used to summon the citizens to public assemblies. When an emergency struck, the bells would be rung *a stormo*; in other words, with a tremendous discordant clattering which brought the citizen militia hurrying to their posts. When the French King Charles VIII threatened Florence in 1494, declaring he would sound his trumpets to signal the attack on the city, the Florentines retorted, 'If you sound your trumpets we will ring our bells.'

From that concept there developed the quite untranslatable idea of *campanilismo*. Roughly, this means excessive attachment to the city (or even the parish) of one's birth. The concept of local patriotism is still strong and takes its most extreme form in the city of Siena, which is divided into 17 parishes, or *contrade*, each named after a bird or an animal. Each of the *contrade* has its own church, its own social centre, its own museum, and its own banner or *gonfalone*. Each has an open-air shrine where the symbol of the *contrade* is erected.

Competition between the *contrade* can be seen at its most intense at the city's celebrated Palio (*see pp148–9*), the bareback horse race between jockeys from each of the parishes, that takes place in summer.

The towering campanile of Florence's cathedral

Firenze (Florence)

Seen from the surrounding hills, Florence seems the perfect example of a romantic Italian city. The warm red-gold roofs nestling in the bowl of the hills, the silver ribbon of the River Arno winding through, the enormous cathedral presiding majestically over its flock, the stern tower of the Palazzo Vecchio soaring up as guardian – all these come together harmoniously to make an enchanting picture.

Fortress city

Despite this, on entering the city itself the first impression is often one of claustrophobia. This is partly due to Florence's history. It was one of the most democratic – but also one of the most turbulent – of Italian city-states, with factions endlessly fighting for dominance. Those who could afford it turned their homes into fortresses which still give a grim appearance to the narrow streets. Occasionally, when the great street door of one of these palaces opens, you may catch a glimpse of a walled garden or a courtyard within, hinting that the dour exterior does not tell the whole story – but, for the most part, Florentine buildings do seem very austere and forbidding.

Modern Florence is also a booming industrial city with a population of just over 380,000. The historic centre inevitably comes under pressure, particularly from traffic. Florentines argue that this is the price you pay for a city that remains very much alive.

Although the city is one of the world's major tourist attractions, drawing in two million people annually, it is still a working city. Even in the historic centre you will find small workshops where furniture is made or bicycles are repaired, side by side with four-star hotels or luxury jewellers.

Mercantile city

Florence has always been like this. In the Middle Ages and the Renaissance Florence owed its great wealth, the factor which allowed it to become the major cultural capital of Europe, not to some all-powerful prince but to its workers, merchants and bankers who built upon the foundations of a thriving wool and textile trade. So confident were foreign traders in the wealth and integrity of Florentine merchants that their gold coin was accepted as a common European currency. That coin was called the 'florino' after the city's Roman name Florentia, which appeared on the obverse. The name 'florin' entered most European languages.

The Florentine virtues during the great formative years of the city were the virtues of merchants – prudence and restraint. Even so, they lavished superb works of art on their sacred buildings and created several big set pieces which every visitor comes to see: the Duomo (Cathedral), the Piazza della Signoria and the Ponte Vecchio. These are usually as crowded as a railway station in the rush hour, and the visitor who sees only these areas may well carry away a rather jaundiced view of the city. If you have time, however, you only need to turn down one of the narrow streets, whose width and course has remained unchanged for centuries, to find the real life of the city.

Galleria dell' Accademia (The Academy Gallery)

The Academy was founded by a group of artists in 1563, the first school of art in Europe. It is now the Florentine School of Art. The Academy Gallery was founded by Grand Duke Pietro Leopoldo in 1784 to house casts and models used by the students. At the entrance to the gallery, on Via Ricasoli, you will almost certainly find a long queue, for the Accademia houses Michelangelo's *David,* one of the top attractions of Florence.

Michelangelo was only 26 when he completed this important piece of work. The statue is carved from a single block of Carrara marble that had been

rejected by other sculptors and had lain around for over 40 years before Michelangelo got to work on it. It was finished in 1504 and, like so much Florentine art, it had a political purpose: *David* signifies the Republic triumphing over the Goliath of tyranny. The statue was originally placed in the Piazza della Signoria; in 1873 it was moved to the Accademia and a copy was installed in its place. The *David* has virtually become a mascot for Florence, but it has not been universally admired. The 19th-century English essayist, William Hazlitt, described it as 'like an

Brunelleschi's soaring cathedral dome – the tallest structure in Florence

Florence city plan

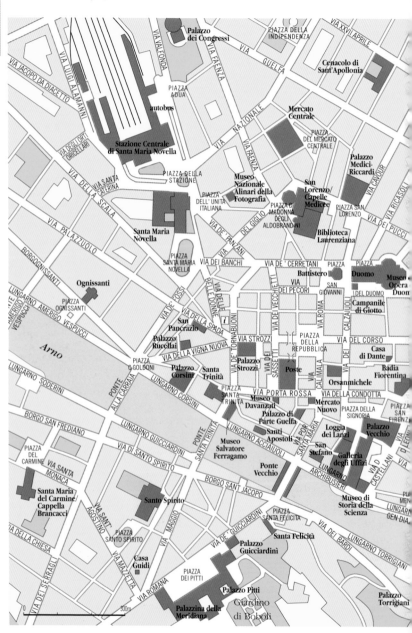

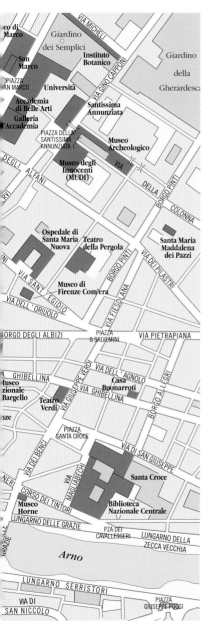

awkward overgrown actor at one of our minor theatres, without his clothes'.

In the same room are Michelangelo's four *Slaves* or *Prisoners*. Unlike *David*, which is finished to such a chill perfection as to leave little room for the imagination, the *Slaves* are unfinished and deeply poignant. Each giant figure, contorted in despair, seems to be trying to break free from the block of marble which imprisons it. You can still see the marks of the chisel which slowly shaped the figure on each block. Originally intended for the immense tomb of Pope Julius II in Rome, Michelangelo worked on them between 1521 and 1523. There has been endless debate about whether they really are unfinished works, and whether Michelangelo intended to leave them like that, to symbolise the soul escaping from the body.

Michelangelo's work dominates, but there is much else to see in the Accademia, including magnificent 16th-century tapestries and paintings ranging from the 13th to 18th centuries, including work by Perugino, Taddeo Gaddi and Filippino Lippi. Finally, the Accademia also houses a small museum of musical instruments, to which admission is included in the regular ticket price.

V Ricasoli 60. Tel: (055) 238 8609; www. firenzemusei.it/00_english/accademia. Open: Tue–Sun 8.15am–6.50pm (until 10pm Fri in summer). Admission charge. Advance booking tel: (055) 294 883. Nearby: Museo di San Marco.

The Renaissance

The Renaissance in Italy is generally assumed to have begun in the early 15th century in Florence – but what exactly was it? Scholars have been debating the question for over 100 years and are likely to continue to do so. Some argue that there was no such thing as 'the Renaissance' and that the period was simply one more evolutionary stage in the continuum of European history. Others argue that 'the' Renaissance was actually 'a' renaissance – in other words, one of many, just like the earlier ones that took place in Carolingian Europe in the 8th and 9th centuries and in France in the 12th century.

Where the Italian Renaissance differs is that people at the time knew that something remarkable was happening, that a profound redirection of thought was taking place. The great scholar Petrarch, writing in the 1350s, said, 'I stand as a man between two worlds.' The word 'rebirth' itself was coined while the process was happening and the word first appeared in print in 1550 when the Florentine art historian, Giorgio Vasari, claimed that his book, *Lives of the Most Excellent Painters, Sculptors and Architects*, would help readers 'to recognise more easily the progress of art's rebirth (*rinascita*)'.

What Vasari meant was that Florentine artists were involved in a revival of the ideas of ancient Greece and Rome, which were then being

Ghiberti's golden Baptistery doors in Florence

Detail from Ghirlandaio's *Nativity* in Santa Trinità church

rediscovered in long-lost manuscripts. This was later extended to include first architecture, and then what we now call science and technology. In 1855 a French historian picked up the idea of a rebirth of classical ideas but translated it into French, and thus as 'Renaissance' it has gone down in history.

In many a Tuscan art gallery, especially those whose paintings are arranged chronologically, it is possible to follow the new trend in art as the formal religious paintings of the Middle Ages gradually give way to paintings of mythological subjects, scenes from daily life, or paintings that are still religious in context but more realistic in the portrayal of

human emotions. The best gallery in which to see this development is the Uffizi in Florence (*see pp49–53*). In architecture the Renaissance is evident in the change from the Gothic buildings of the Middle Ages to classical structures derived from the study of Roman architecture. The Rucellai Palace in Florence is a good example of the latter. In literature, writers such as Petrarch and Boccaccio turned away from an endless preoccupation with theology, 'the study of God', to humanism, 'the study of man'. These three trends put together changed the face of Tuscany and, within a few years, had sparked off similar movements in many parts of Europe.

Badia Fiorentina
(Abbey of Florence)

It is said that Dante used to haunt this ancient church (founded in 978, rebuilt in 1285) in order to feast his eyes on Beatrice, the girl he idolised in *The Divine Comedy*. He would still recognise the Romanesque campanile, although much of the church was rebuilt again in 1627. At first sight the interior seems empty and uninteresting, but there are two superb works of art. On the left-hand wall in front of the altar is the tomb of Ugo, Margrave of Tuscany (died 1001), son of Willa, who founded the abbey in memory of her husband, Uberto. The tomb itself is a Renaissance masterpiece, sculpted by Mino da Fiesole during 1469–81. The other great work is a painting, *The Madonna Appearing to St Bernard* (1485), by Filippino Lippi. To the right of the choir a staircase leads to the Chiostro degli Aranci (the Cloister of the Oranges) where the monks once grew orange trees. The walls are decorated with 15th-century frescoes on the life of St Bernard.

Via Dante Alighieri. Tel: (055) 287 389. Open: Tue–Thur 5–7pm. Abbey under long-term restoration – check times locally. Free admission.

Nearby: Museo Nazionale del Bargello.

Battistero San Giovanni
(Baptistery)

Built some time between the 5th and 8th centuries on Roman foundations, this is the oldest surviving building in Florence. Indeed, as late as the 15th century, the Florentines claimed that it had once been a temple to Mars, founded by Julius Caesar. This is the sacred building most revered by the citizens of Florence. According to custom, on 21 March all children born in the city over the previous 12 months were brought here to be baptised.

The elegant green and white marble cladding of the exterior was added between the 11th and 13th centuries, and it served as a model for other Florentine churches. The interior is richly decorated, incorporating Roman columns and capitals. The self-confident Florentines did not hesitate to call on the artists of other cities to embellish their beloved Baptistery: the Byzantine-style mosaic in the ceiling is probably the work of Venetian artists while the decoration of the font is Pisan. The only other object in the interior is the exquisite tomb, designed by Donatello, of the 'antipope' John

The Bargello's stately courtyard (*see pp56–8*)

XXIII (Baldassarre Cossa) who was deposed in 1414.

Beautiful though the interior is, the three sets of bronze double doors are what set the Baptistery apart from any other building in the world. The South Doors are the oldest. They were made by Andrea Pisano around 1330. The 20 panels at the top tell the story of Florence's patron saint, St John the Baptist, while the bottom eight panels show the Virtues.

The North and East Doors are among the most important objects in the history of modern art, for they mark a key moment in the development of Renaissance techniques, such as naturalistic perspective.

In 1402 the wealthy Guild of Cloth Merchants of Florence decided to celebrate the city's delivery from plague by commissioning a new set of doors, the North Doors. A competition was organised – another 'first' in art history – and seven leading artists were invited to submit a panel on the same subject, the Sacrifice of Isaac.

Two artists, Lorenzo Ghiberti and Filippo Brunelleschi, were eventually judged to be the joint winners (their original panels can be seen in the Bargello). The Guild suggested they work together, but Brunelleschi refused and went off, in high dudgeon, to study classical architecture in Rome.

The 25-year-old Ghiberti thus began his single-handed work on the doors; he started in 1403 – and did not finish until 21 years later. The Guild were so

The octagonal Baptistery (left) is the oldest surviving building in Florence

pleased with his work that they immediately commissioned another set of doors for the eastern portal. Ghiberti spent the next 27 years on these (1425–52).

Both sets of doors are staggering in their detail and execution. The North Doors consist of 28 panels surrounded by Gothic quatrefoils, representing the Life of Christ and the Evangelists in a manner which is far removed from the formalism of the Middle Ages.

The East Doors (facing the cathedral) consist of only ten panels but these are the doors which Michelangelo described as the 'Gates of Paradise'.

The panels you see now are casts of the originals (which have been removed for cleaning and subsequent display in the Museo dell'Opera del Duomo; four panels are currently on display). Even so, the reproductions clearly show Ghiberti's genius, and his work is better seen here than in a museum. The panels illustrate in a lively, realistic style Old Testament scenes such as the Creation of Adam and Eve. Ghiberti also departed from tradition by including portraits of his contemporaries, in the guise of prophets and sibyls, around the frames. He even put his self-portrait there: he is the fourth down on the right-hand side, a balding man with a rather self-satisfied smile (the figure next to him is his father).

Piazza San Giovanni/Piazza del Duomo. Tel: (055) 230 2885; www.operaduomo.firenze.it. Open: Mon–Sat noon–7pm, Sun & religious holidays 8.30am–2pm. Admission charge.

Giotto's elegant campanile

Campanile di Giotto (Giotto's Bell Tower)

Although universally known as 'Giotto's Tower', Giotto was responsible only for the first storey, begun in 1334. The rest of the work was undertaken by Andrea Pisano between 1337 and 1342, and completed by Francesco Talenti during 1348–59. The extraordinary multi-coloured marble and Gothic tracery ensures that the tower stands out among the surrounding sober buildings, and only the cathedral and Baptistery can compete with it. Like so many of Florence's outdoor sculptures, the originals of the panels which decorated the tower are now in a museum, the Museo dell'Opera del Duomo. The ascent to the top of the tower, a stiff 414-step climb, provides a spectacular view.

Piazza del Duomo. Tel: (055) 230 2885; www.operaduomo.firenze.it. Bell tower: open daily 8.30am–7.30pm. Last admission 6.50pm. Admission charge. Nearby: Duomo, Battistero, Museo dell'Opera del Duomo.

Cappella Brancacci (Brancacci Chapel)

In 1424 Felice Brancacci, a wealthy Florentine diplomat, decided to follow the fashionable trend and pay for the decoration of a chapel in his local church – Santa Maria del Carmine. He chose an established artist, Masolino da Panicale (1383–1447). Masolino's 22-year-old assistant was called Tommaso di Ser Giovanni di Mone Cassai (1401–28); the Florentines nicknamed him Masaccio – meaning 'Hulking or Loutish Tom' – presumably because of his appearance. The assistant rapidly became the master and he created a series of frescoes which do for painting what Ghiberti's Baptistery doors do for sculpture: they mark the moment when the Renaissance broke free from the Middle Ages.

Most of the panels tell the life of St Peter, turning him into a real person instead of the remote, god-like figure of earlier art. Perhaps the most famous of all Masaccio's scenes is the *Expulsion of Adam and Eve*, which makes a complete break with every previous presentation of the subject. Adam has buried his face in his hands in utter despair while Eve is screaming in terror. It is interesting to compare this treatment with Masolino's depiction of the same subject on the opposite wall. The frescoes, after long neglect, were brilliantly restored between 1984 and 1990.

Santa Maria del Carmine, Piazza del Carmine 14. Tel: (055) 276 8224. Open: Mon & Wed–Sat 10am–5pm, Sun & public holidays 1–5pm. Admission charge. Nearby: Santo Spirito. Reservation required.

DANTE ALIGHIERI (1265–1321)

When Dante wrote his epic poem *The Divine Comedy* in the Tuscan dialect instead of in the universal scholarly language of Latin, he gave the 'people's language' a tremendous boost. His three-part poem describes his journey through Hell, Purgatory and Paradise, and is a curious mixture of political propaganda, mysticism – and personal spite: he placed his enemies in 'Hell' and devised suitable eternal punishments for their 'sins'. Dante was exiled from Florence in 1302 as a result of one of the city's many political upheavals. For the rest of his life he wandered round the courts and monasteries of northern Italy. He died in Ravenna and was buried there.

Florence sends an annual gift of oil to Ravenna for the lamps around his tomb. Off and on there is talk of returning Dante's remains to Florence, but that is unlikely ever to happen.

Strolling across the River Arno; the spiritual side of Florence

Heaven, Hell, Dante and Florence

Casa Buonarroti (Michelangelo's House)

Michelangelo (whose surname was Buonarroti) bought this house in 1508 but never lived in it, regarding it simply as a useful investment. It was his nephew Leonardo who, after inheriting the house in 1564, began to develop it as a kind of shrine to the memory of his famous uncle. In 1612 Michelangelo Buonarroti the Younger extended the house and commissioned a number of artists to create imaginary pictures of the life of the great man. The house first opened in the form of a Michelangelo Museum in the mid-19th century.

Despite its tenuous connection with Michelangelo himself, the museum provides an invaluable insight into his life and work. The most important exhibits are on the first floor, including Michelangelo's earliest known work, the sculptural panel called *The Madonna of the Staircase* (1491).

There is also a wooden model of Michelangelo's design for the façade of San Lorenzo, though this was never built.
Via Ghibellina 70. Tel: (055) 241 752; www.casabuonarroti.it. Open: Wed–Mon 9.30am–2pm. Admission charge. Nearby: Santa Croce.

Casa di Dante (Dante's House)

Although this is an entirely modern reconstruction built on an historic site, it is definitely well worth a visit as an honest attempt to re-create a 13th-century house. On display are editions of *The Divine Comedy* as well as Botticelli's illustrations of the famous poem. Whether or not Dante was born in a house actually on this site, this is certainly his home ground. Just across

the narrow street is the church of **Santa Margherita de'Cerchi** where, it is said, Dante was married, while nearby is the Badia Fiorentina (*see p32*), the parish church of his great love, Beatrice.
Via Santa Margherita.
Tel: (055) 219 416;
www.museocasadidante.it. Open:
Tue–Fri 10am–6pm (5pm winter), Sat 10am–1pm, 1st Sun 10am–4pm, 2nd & 3rd Sun 10am–1pm. Closed: 4th Sun. Santa Margherita de'Cerchi: open Mon–Sat 9am–noon, 3–6.30pm, Sun 9am–noon. Admission charge.

Churches
Cappelle Medicee (Medici Chapels)
Although attached to San Lorenzo Church, the Medici Chapels have a separate entrance in the Piazza Madonna degli Aldobrandini. The grandest of the chapels, the Cappella dei Principi, is entered first. This was commissioned by the Grand Duke, Cosimo I, and designed by Buontalenti, who began work in 1605. The vast marble mausoleum, designed to display the wealth and power of the later Medici, was not completed until 1737. The pavement and walls are inlaid with coloured marbles and semi-precious stones – lapis lazuli, mother-of-pearl, coral and porphyry.

The Sagrestia Nuova (New Sacristy) was commissioned by the Medici Pope Leo X and the contrast between this serene, harmonious chapel and its vulgar neighbour is total. This is not

Michelangelo's *Dawn and Dusk* at the Medici Chapels

surprising, for both the sculptures and the architecture of the sacristy are the work of Michelangelo (1520–34). Ironically, the two tombs which carry four of his most famous sculptures commemorate little-known members of the Medici family. On the right is the sarcophagus of Giuliano, Duke of Nemours, who died in 1516. The figures which crown the tomb are known as Day and Night. Opposite is the tomb of Lorenzo, Duke of Urbino (died 1519), crowned by the figures of Dawn and Dusk.

In the little room behind the altar in the sacristy, perspex sheeting covers some rough sketches in charcoal made on the wall by Michelangelo and discovered in 1975. He probably hid in this room during the time that the Medici reconquered the city in 1531.

A small chamber below has yet more sketches which were discovered after the great flood of 1966.
Piazza Madonna degli Aldobrandini.
Tel: (055) 238 8602;
www.firenzemusei.it/00_english/medicee.
Open: daily 8.15am–5pm, except Mon &
alternate Sun. Admission charge.
Advance booking tel: (055) 294 883.
Nearby: San Lorenzo.

Ognissanti (All Saints)

Ognissanti was the parish church of Amerigo Vespucci, the man after whom the continent of America was named. Founded in 1259, the church was completely rebuilt in 1627 in the Baroque style then in fashion, although

THE VESPUCCI FAMILY

The Vespucci were a very wealthy family of merchants, who traded widely, dealing mostly in luxury clothing and wine. However, despite their wealth, they were closely identified with the predominantly working-class quarter where the parish church of Ognissanti is located.

Amerigo (1451–1512) worked for the Medici as an agent in Spain. In 1499 Amerigo made a voyage – for which he came to be known over the centuries – across the Atlantic, as a result of which he proved that Columbus had discovered a 'new world' and not the eastern shores of India as he had supposed.

The first maps of the new world were based on Vespucci's account of his voyage, published in 1504, and because of this the lands previously known as 'Mundus Novus' were called 'America' – after the Latin version of Vespucci's Christian name.

the campanile is medieval. The interior of the church is richly decorated in the rather lush manner of the period but contains work by Botticelli (who is buried here) and Ghirlandaio. The Vespucci family tomb is below the second altar on the right. Ghirlandaio's painting over the altar, the *Madonna of Mercy,* supposedly contains a portrait of Amerigo himself – he is the boy peering from behind the man in the dark cloak. Above the altar opposite is Botticelli's *St Augustine* (1480). Another work by Ghirlandaio is in the convent next to the church (entry through the cloister); the refectory holds his great fresco of *The Last Supper* (1480).
Via Borgognissanti.
Tel: (055) 239 8700;

www.polomuseale.firenze.it/english/ musei/ognissanti. Church: open daily 9am–12.30pm & 4–6.30pm. Closed: Fri morning and during religious services. Refectory: open Mon, Tue & Sat 9am–noon. Free admission.

Orsanmichele
(St Michael by the Garden)

The Italian habit of truncating words and running them together has given this church its unusual name, which contains a clue to Florence's past. Between the 9th and 13th centuries there was a garden here (*orto* in Italian)

with a church alongside called San Michele ad Hortum (St Michael by the garden). This church was later replaced by a loggia which was used as a trading hall. In 1380, the loggia was enclosed and two upper storeys added, giving the building its present odd appearance, for it looks more like a tower than a church. At this point, the ground floor was once again used as a church, and the upper floors as an emergency grain store.

Each of the city's guilds was given responsibility for decorating one of the niches in the outside wall of the church.

Bernardo Daddi's radiant *Madonna and Child* framed by angels in Orsanmichele church

From this developed the present astonishing display of statuary, as the guilds strove to outdo each other. Some of the statues have been moved to museums and replaced by copies. Among the most important are: (east side) Ghiberti's *John the Baptist* (1416), the first full-size Renaissance statue in bronze, and *Doubting Thomas* by Verrocchio (1483); (north side) *St George* (1416) by Donatello (a copy, the original is in the Bargello) and Nanni di Banco's *Four Crowned Saints* (1415); (west side) Ghiberti's *St Matthew* (1422), and *St Eligius* (1414) by Nanni di Banco (the bas-relief below shows some of the saint's miracles); (south side) Donatello's *St Mark* (1411).

The interior is as oddly shaped as the exterior and very dark. Its outstanding

Rich frescoes by Taddeo Gaddi at Santa Croce

feature is the tabernacle in glass and marble by Orcagna (1348–59) which glows like an immense jewel in artificial light. Access to the upper storeys is by a footbridge from the Palazzo dell'Arte della Lana opposite.
Via Arte della Lana. Tel: (055) 284 944; www.polomuseale.firenze.it/english/ musei/orsanmichele. Church: open daily 9am–noon, 4–6pm. Museum: open Tue–Sun 10am–5pm. Free admission.

GIOTTO DI BONDONE

Giotto (1266–1337) was the first artist in medieval Italy who broke away from the formality of Byzantine-inspired art. Giotto painted his figures and landscapes in a very realistic style, thus laying the foundation for the art of the Renaissance period.

Giotto was born in a village near Florence, the son of a peasant farmer. According to Vasari, Giotto learned to draw as a shepherd boy – while watching flocks of sheep in the pastures – by scratching pictures of sheep into the rocks: hence the idea that Giotto's naturalism came from his study of nature. Even if we allow for the fact that Giotto was helped by numerous pupils and assistants, his output was astonishing. Giotto's most famous (though now disputed) work is the St Francis fresco cycle in Assisi, but his work is also to be found in Rome, Naples, Bologna, Padua and Florence.

Santa Croce (Holy Cross)
Begun in 1294 and intended to be one of the largest churches in Christendom, the basilica of Santa Croce was finally completed in the 19th century when the façade was paid for by the British benefactor, Sir Francis Sloane. Built for the purpose of preaching, the church has a large square at the front in case of overflow. The vast interior features nine chapels at the eastern end, each one named after one of the immensely wealthy banking families of the city

who paid for its mural decorations. These frescoes, including some by Giotto, are among the most important medieval works of art in Florence.

The church is also Florence's Pantheon – the burial place of the city's outstanding men. Starting at the main entrance from Piazza Santa Croce, the first tomb on the left-hand side (north aisle) is that of Galileo, who was originally refused burial within the main church, but whose body was moved here in 1737. On the opposite side (the south aisle) the first tomb is that of Michelangelo, who died in Rome in 1564. Next is Dante's cenotaph. It is empty because Dante never returned to his native city after he was exiled in 1302; when he died he was buried in Ravenna.

Just beyond Dante's 19th-century cenotaph is an 18th-century memorial to Niccolò Machiavelli (died 1527), author of *The Prince*, and Secretary to the Republic before it was overthrown by the Medici. Between the two, on the nearby nave pillar, is a pulpit by Benedetto da Maiano (1476), regarded as one of the most perfect of the Renaissance. Then comes a beautiful *Annunciation* in gilded limestone by Donatello (around 1435), while high up on the wall just beyond is the faultless Renaissance tomb of Leonardo Bruni (died 1444), the scholar who wrote the first history of Florence.

The two chapels on the right-hand side of the high altar are the Bardi and Peruzzi chapels, both decorated by Giotto and his pupils in the 1330s. The frescoes have deteriorated because Giotto painted on dry plaster, instead of wet, and the paint eventually flaked off in places. Their condition became so

The magnificent Santa Croce Church rises above a sea of red roofs

poor that they were whitewashed over in the 18th century and forgotten for over 150 years before being restored in 1959. The Bardi chapel (next to the altar) contains scenes from the life of St Francis of Assisi; though not as striking as Giotto's famous frescoes on the same subject in Assisi, scenes such as the *Death of St Francis* show the artist's mastery in depicting human emotions. The fifth chapel to the left of the high altar (the Bardi di Vernio) was frescoed by Giotto's follower, Maso di Banco, with *Scenes from the Life of St Sylvester* (late 1360s).

Off to the right-hand (south) side of the main altar is a passageway that leads to the sacristy, dominated by a tremendous 14th-century *Crucifixion* by Taddeo Gaddi.

Housed in the old monastic buildings adjoining the basilica is the Museo dell'Opera di Santa Croce with works by Cimabue, Donatello and Orcagna.

Basilica, Piazza Santa Croce. Tel: (055) 244 6105; www.santacroce.firenze.it. Museum and church: open Mon–Sat 9.30am–5.30pm, Sun & Holy Days 1–5.30pm. Single admission charge to visit church and museum.

San Lorenzo (St Lawrence)

Looked at from outside, it is difficult to imagine that this battered, unfinished church situated in a rumbustious and inelegant marketplace was the 'family church' of the wealthy and powerful Medici. Inside, it is a different story.

Designed by Brunelleschi and built between 1419 and 1469, it was the very first church to be built in Renaissance style in Florence. Its details are important not just in the history of art but also because they relate to the Medici and reflect the history of Florence over three centuries.

The great nave is a cool and classically harmonious work in grey stone. High up on their individual pillars are two great bronze pulpits partly executed by Donatello (1455–66), the last of his works and commissioned by his great friend Cosimo de' Medici. Just beyond, a multi-coloured marble roundel in the floor marks the spot where Cosimo himself lies buried. He died in 1464 and his epitaph simply says '*Pater Patriae*' (Father of the Fatherland), the title bestowed upon him by the city council after his death, and the same title once given to Cicero by the Roman senate.

In the crypt below, the very last of the Medici, Anna Maria Ludovica, also lies buried. On her death in 1743 her will revealed that she had left

San Lorenzo Church

everything the Medici owned to the citizens of Florence, which explains why the city is such a treasure house of art today.

On the left of the high altar is the entrance to the Sagrestia Vecchia (the Old Sacristy). Built by Brunelleschi during 1421–9, and decorated with reliefs by Donatello from 1434 to 1443, this contains the tomb of the founder of the Medici family wealth, the banker Giovanni di Bicci de' Medici (died 1429) and that of Donatello himself. *Piazza San Lorenzo. Tel: (055) 264 5184. Open: Mon–Sat 10am–5pm, Mar–Oct Sun 1.30–5.30pm. Admission charge.*

Santa Maria Novella (New Church of St Mary)

This enormous church was built in the late 13th century by the Dominicans. They were proud of the pun on their name – '*Domini Canes*' (Hounds of the Lord) – for it was they who hounded heretics through the Inquisition. Thus it is that the frescoes in the Cappellone degli Spagnoli (the Spanish Chapel) in the cloister show the Dominicans as black and white dogs, those being the colours of their habits. It was in this church, from the pulpit designed by Donatello, that Galileo was denounced for teaching that the earth went round the sun and not the other way round.

Santa Maria Novella is particularly famous for its frescoes. On the left-hand wall of the nave is *The Trinity* by Masaccio. Painted in 1428, a year or so

The series of frescoes by Ghirlandaio at Santa Maria Novella

before his death at the tender age of 27, this was one of the first paintings to make full use of the new science of perspective.

Behind the high altar is a charming fresco series painted by Ghirlandaio with the help of his assistants, one of whom was the young Michelangelo. The frescoes depict scenes from the lives of the Virgin and of St John the Baptist, but almost all the scenes are set in the Florence of the time, thus providing a marvellous insight into the social life of the 15th-century city. For instance, the women present at the births of St John and the Virgin Mary are ladies of the Tornabuoni family who commissioned the frescoes.

The Medici

The Medici family ruled the city of Florence almost continuously for over 300 years, from 1434 until the death of the last of the Medici, Anna Maria Ludovica, in 1743. At first they wielded power but without holding any official office or title.

The Medici coat of arms

Later, their position of absolute power was acknowledged when Alessandro was crowned the first Duke of Florence in 1530 and Cosimo I was made the first Grand Duke of Tuscany in 1569.

Two of the most important members of the family were Cosimo 'Il Vecchio' ('the elder'), who ruled from 1434 until his death in 1464, and his brilliant grandson Lorenzo 'Il Magnifico' ('the Magnificent') who ruled from 1469 until he died in 1492. Cosimo used his enormous wealth as a banker to build such monuments as San Lorenzo Church and the Monastery of San Marco. He himself was a scholar and he paid for other scholars to collect and translate ancient Greek and Roman manuscripts, including the works of Plato and Cicero; by this means he was instrumental in encouraging renewed interest in the classics, one of the defining characteristics of the Humanist age.

Lorenzo assumed the leadership of the family and the city at the age of 20 when his father (Piero the Gouty) succumbed to an early death in 1469. Lorenzo was reluctant to take up the reins of power but, as he said frankly, 'It fares ill in Florence with any who

Verrocchio's portrait of Cosimo 'the elder'

possess wealth without any share of the government.'

Lorenzo soon proved himself a worthy and able leader in the same mould as his grandfather, Cosimo. Though physically an unattractive man, with a sallow skin, a great beaky nose and a harsh squeaky voice, he was immensely popular among all classes. He was himself a gifted statesman, poet, musician and philosopher, and he was capable of recognising genius in others – among the many artists whom he encouraged was the young Michelangelo. His death at the early age of 43 was a tragedy for Florence.

The Medici coat of arms, displayed in the many Tuscan cities conquered by the family, as well as in Florence itself, consists of six balls or pills (*palle*) on a shield – probably a reference to the origin of the family name, from *medico* or 'physician'.

The cloisters to the left of the church also have a spectacular range of frescoes and form part of the church museum. Several of the scenes on the life of Noah were painted by Paolo Uccello, who was literally obsessed by the mathematics of linear perspective, spending hour upon hour making complex calculations. He used a green pigment, giving a ghostly hue to his awesome picture *Universal Deluge* with its tragic victims (c.1430).

Piazza Santa Maria Novella. Tel: (055) 264 5184; www.smn.it. Church: open Mon–Thur & Sat 9am–5pm, Fri, Sun & Feast Days 1–5pm. Admission charge. Museum: open Mon–Thur & Sat 9am–5pm, Sun 9am–2pm. Closed: Fri.

The Duomo, a prominent landmark

Museum and cloisters, tel: (055) 282 187. Admission charge.

Santa Trinità (Holy Trinity)

Founded in 1092 but rebuilt between 1258 and 1280, Santa Trinità is famous for a miraculous crucifix and vivid pictures of social life in 15th-century Florence. The crucifix is in the chapel on the right of the altar and, legend has it, nodded approval to a young man who forgave his brother's murderer.

The adjoining Sassetti Chapel has frescoes by Ghirlandaio. As with his frescoes which can be found in Santa Maria Novella, these scenes incorporate contemporary people and settings. On the altar wall are scenes from the life of St Francis set in the Piazza della Signoria and in Piazza Santa Trinità, while the figures include Lorenzo de' Medici ('the Magnificent'), his sons and their tutors.

Piazza Santa Trinità. Tel: (055) 216 912. Open: Mon–Sat 8am–noon, 4–6pm, Sun 4–6pm. Free admission.

Santo Spirito (Holy Spirit)

Santo Spirito is well worth a visit because it is the last major work of the great Renaissance architect Filippo Brunelleschi. He prepared a model for the church in 1428, and work was in progress by the time of his death in 1446. The façade was never completed, hence its disappointing front, but the perfect classical harmony of the interior is as Brunelleschi intended. There are paintings by Verrocchio and Filippino Lippi in the transepts.

Piazza Santo Spirito. Tel: (055) 210 030.
Open: Sat Apr–Oct 9am–5pm, Nov–Mar
9am–1.30pm. Admission charge.

Duomo Santa Maria del Fiore (Cathedral)

The first sight of the exterior of the
Cathedral of Santa Maria del Fiore
(Holy Mary of the Flowers) may come
as a shock because its multi-coloured
marbles hover on the brink of an almost
fairground garishness. In all, marbles of
three different colours have been used:
white from Carrara, red from the
Maremma and green from Prato.

The cathedral was begun in 1296 as
a deliberate challenge to the great
cathedrals then rising in Pisa and Siena:
the Florentines announcing that their
cathedral would be the greatest
building in the world, 'surpassing
anything built by the Greeks and
Romans'. The first architect, Arnolfo di
Cambio, drew up a plan, and
construction work went well for over
100 years. The building was nearly
complete by 1418 – all except for the
enormous dome. Nobody had any idea
how the huge space was to be covered
without incurring a vast expense in
timber and scaffolding.

After endless anxious debate, the
authorities decided to let Filippo
Brunelleschi build the dome – though
not without some hesitation because
Brunelleschi declined to say how he
would accomplish the task, except that
he promised no scaffolding would be
used. Brunelleschi succeeded, using a

Looking out from the top of the cathedral
dome provides a new perspective on Florence

cantilevered system, to raise what was
then the biggest dome in the world. It
took 16 years to complete and even
today is surpassed in size only by
St Peter's in Rome. The lantern was
planned by Brunelleschi but added
only in 1461, after his death. It has
stood the test of time despite fears that
its weight would bring the whole dome
crashing down.

As with so many Florentine churches,
the façade was left unfinished. The
present confection was made in 1887
and is already in need of renovation.
The marble was obtained by explosives,
rather than the traditional method of
sawing. Critics say this weakened its
molecular structure, causing the façade
to deteriorate.

Firenze (Florence)

A side view of the Duomo

The interior of the building is huge – contemporary reports claim that at least 10,000 people crowded in to hear the sermons of Savonarola. The proportions are majestic but the colouring is a rather depressing brown, coming to life only on feast days when the great columns are hung with crimson banners.

Ironically, two of the most prominent works of art are portraits of mercenary soldiers; both are on the left-hand (northern) wall of the nave. They depict Niccolò da Tolentino and the Englishman Sir John Hawkwood who became Captain General of Florence in 1377 (*see pp100–101*). The Florentines had promised the latter a memorial in the form of an equestrian statue but they fobbed off his heirs with this fresco (1436) by Paolo Uccello instead. Uccello used his great skill in

perspective to create this chiaroscuro picture, which gives the appearance of a three-dimensional statue.

Just beyond, on the pillar on the right, is a painting of Dante. After Dante's death the Florentines atoned for his exile by instituting a series of public readings of his work in the cathedral at Easter. The background to this painting shows 'Paradise' and 'Inferno' as Dante envisaged them; also, the major buildings of 15th-century Florence.

It is possible to ascend the 463 steps to the summit of the **cathedral dome** but this should only be attempted by those with a very good head for heights; the gallery is narrow and the balustrade is only waist high. The **crypt** is also open to the public (separate admission charge), and contains Roman remains and the foundations of

Santa Reparata Church, originally built in the 4th century but demolished to make way for the cathedral in 1296. Here, too, you can see Brunelleschi's simple tomb; he is the only person ever to have been buried in the cathedral. *Piazza del Duomo. Tel: (055) 230 2885; www.operaduomo.firenze.it.*
Open: Mon–Sat 10am–5pm (except Thur 4.30pm and Sat 4.45pm), Sun 1.30–4.45pm. Free admission.
Dome, tel: (055) 230 2885.
Open: Mon–Sat 8.30am–7pm, Sun 8.30am–2pm. Admission charge.
Crypt, tel: (055) 230 2885.
Open: Mon–Sat 10am–5pm. Admission charge.

Galleria degli Uffizi (Uffizi Gallery)

The building was designed by Vasari in 1560 as a suite of administrative offices (*uffizi*) for Cosimo I. Construction continued until 1586 and the gallery encloses three sides of what was once a street leading from Piazza della Signoria down to the river. Cosimo's heirs, most notably Francesco I, decided to display their ever-expanding collection in the 'offices', and in 1737 Anna Maria Ludovica, the last of the Medici, bequeathed the collection and the building to the people of Florence.

Successors to the Medici continued to add to the Uffizi collection and works are still being acquired. In the reception area, for instance, there is a startlingly modern work, *The Battle of San Martino,* by Carrado Caylis (1936).

Today the gallery contains the world's greatest collection of Florentine Renaissance paintings, covering the whole history of the period. It also possesses a rich variety of works from other countries and periods – it has, for instance, some important works by Rembrandt. Other galleries may have a larger number of paintings, but few other galleries have so many world-famous works of art that simply demand to be looked at.

The risk of suffering from mental indigestion is a hazard throughout Italy, particularly high in Florence, and virtually unavoidable in the Uffizi, unless you are selective. The best survival technique is to choose a dozen or so paintings or sculptures (assisted by the guidebook obtainable in the reception area) for detailed study – and resist the rest.

Though the entrance fee makes this one of the most expensive galleries in Italy, there is always a queue at the entrance in the high tourist season; advance booking is strongly recommended. Most of the gallery is on the third floor; access is by means of Vasari's monumental staircase (there is a lift for visitors with disabilities). There is an informal one-way system in operation through the gallery, and in the high season it is virtually impossible to retrace your steps in order to have another look because of the crowds. Plans to expand the Uffizi are well under way, and new rooms have opened on the second floor. Despite considerable opposition, expansion of the Uffizi has begun with a new modernist-style exit by architect Arata Isozaki, due to open in 2011.

In May 1993, a car bomb exploded at the back of the west wing of the Uffizi. Although the building's structure remained sound, three paintings were destroyed and some 30 others damaged. The museum's most important works, however, survived untouched.

Highlights of the Uffizi
Reception area

This area has frescoes of famous Florentines by Andrea del Castagno (1421–57), including portraits of Dante and Boccaccio which, though painted posthumously, are based on contemporary portraits and are widely accepted as faithful likenesses.

Rooms 2 and 3

Here you can trace the dawning of the Renaissance through three examples of a *Maestà* (the word means Majesty, and paintings of this type show the Virgin enthroned in heaven, surrounded by saints); they are by Cimabue (c.1240–1302), Duccio di Buoninsegna (c.1260–1320) and Giotto (1266–1337). Another powerful work is the *Annunciation* by Simone Martini (c.1284–1344), all a blaze of gold. The subjects are still formally presented but the Madonna is shown as human and there are glimpses of everyday life in the costumes and buildings depicted.

Room 7

Here are two superb portraits by Piero della Francesca (c.1420–92): Federico da Montefeltro and his wife Battista Sforza. Montefeltro, the Duke of Urbino, was one of the first princes to espouse Renaissance and Humanist values at his court. Nearby is *The Battle of San Romano* by Paolo Uccello (1396–1475), essentially an exercise in the new-found technique of perspective. This is one of three paintings Uccello made on the same subject.

Rooms 8 and 9

Filippo Lippi (1406–69) was, according to Vasari, a rascally drunken protégé of

Detail from Botticelli's *The Birth of Venus*, housed at the Uffizi

the Medici, but he produced ethereal Madonnas, often using his mistress as his model, such as in the *Madonna and Child with Two Angels* and the *Coronation of the Virgin*. Antonio del Pollaiuolo (c.1432–98) dissected corpses to learn about human anatomy, applying what he learned to paintings, as in the two tiny *Labours of Hercules*.

Rooms 10–14

The works of Sandro Botticelli (c.1445–1510) displayed in these rooms are probably the Uffizi's most powerful attractions. In his early life as a protégé of the Medici, Botticelli was obsessed by mythology: the works he painted at this time include the enchanting *Birth of Venus* and the mysterious *Primavera* (Spring) – the same beautiful model appears in both pictures as Venus and as the enigmatically smiling goddess Flora.

Later in life, Botticelli fell under the influence of Savonarola and devoted himself to religious subjects; typical of this phase is the *Adoration of the Magi* in which Botticelli included portraits of the Medici and a self-portrait (he is the figure on the right in a saffron robe looking out of the picture at the viewer). By total contrast, this room also contains the *Adoration of the Shepherds* painted around 1475 by the Flemish painter, Hugo van der Goes. The shepherds in this picture are realistic manual workers and not, as in Botticelli's painting, posing courtiers.

The Uffizi is one of the most expensive galleries in Italy

Room 15

This room contains a painting by Andrea Verrocchio (c.1435–88), the *Baptism of Christ*. Verrocchio's apprentice was Leonardo da Vinci (1452–1519), who painted the angel on the left of the picture and may have painted most of the *Annunciation* in the same room. Nearby hangs Leonardo's unfinished *Adoration of the Magi*.

Room 18

This octagonal room, the Tribuna, is itself an exhibit. Designed in 1584 to hold important Medici treasures – including the *Medici Venus* (1st-century BC Roman copy of a Greek 4th-century BC original) and antique sculptures, including the delightful *Dancing Faun* – the dome is inlaid with mother-of-pearl and the floor made of a semi-precious marble inlay. Also on display are court portraits of the Medici family, among them posthumous portraits of Cosimo II Vecchio by Jacopo Pontormo (1494–1556) and Lorenzo the Magnificent by Giorgio Vasari (1511–74).

Room 20

The Medici's wide-ranging taste is well illustrated by the works of German painters hung in this room. Albrecht Dürer (1471–1528) is represented by the portrait of his father, Lucas Cranach (1472–1553) by his *Adam and Eve*, and (oddly for a family one of whose number, Pope Leo X, excommunicated Luther) his *Portrait of Martin Luther*. It is interesting to compare this picture with the School of Holbein portrait of the English statesman and martyr, Sir Thomas More, in room 22.

Room 25

Michelangelo Buonarroti (1475–1564) is represented here by the stunning *Holy Family*, the only one of his paintings to survive in Florence but one that was enormously influential on the Mannerist artists of the High Renaissance because of its adventurous use of colour and the unusual pose of the Virgin.

Room 26

This room contains a major work by Raphael (1483–1520), his portrait of

the Medici Pope Leo X. The short-sighted pope is shown studying a richly illuminated manuscript while his half-brother, Cardinal Giulio de' Medici (later Pope Clement VII), and Cardinal Luigi de' Rossi stand deferentially alongside him.

Room 28

This contains Titian's sensual and intimate *Venus of Urbino* (1538).

Sala del Caravaggio

Newly opened, this room contains important works by Caravaggio, including his *Sacrifice of Isaac* (1603) and *Medusa* (1595–8).

Corridoio Vasariano (Vasari's Corridor)

After Cosimo I moved across the river to the Pitti Palace, he wanted to be able to walk back and forth between his home and the city centre discreetly – and in safety. From this developed one of the most extraordinary structures in Florence. Vasari built a corridor which, leaving the southeastern corner of the Uffizi, runs on arches high above the pavement along the embankment as far as the Ponte Vecchio; it then soars over the top of the bridge, passes in front of the church of Santa Felicita, and eventually links up with the Pitti Palace. The corridor is used to display a remarkable collection of artists' self-portraits. The corridor is open only periodically, by guided tours. Advance booking is required.

Uffizi Gallery, Piazzale degli Uffizi 6.
Tel: (055) 238 8651;
www.polomuseale.firenze.it/english/
musei/uffizi.
Open: Tue–Sun 8.15am–6.50pm,
July–Sept Tue until 10pm.
Closed: Mon.
Admission charge.
Advance booking: tel: (055) 294 883.
Nearby: Palazzo Vecchio.

Corridoio Vasariano,
information: tel: (055) 294 883.

Museums
Museo Archeologico
(Archaeological Museum)
Housed in a 17th-century palace, the
Palazzo della Crocetta, this vast
collection – which includes exhibits
from ancient Egypt, Greece and Rome
as well as Tuscany – was once
admirably labelled and displayed. The
museum suffered badly in the 1966
flood, and the effects are still being felt.
Some rooms are still closed, and
elsewhere the exhibits are being
rearranged. Sensibly, the authorities
have concentrated on restoring and
displaying the more famous and
popular exhibits, many of which are
again on view in enhanced conditions.

The museum was begun by the
Medici, and the core of the collection
comes from the bequest of the last of
the dynasty, Anna Maria Ludovica.
As a result, the museum has some of
the finest Etruscan treasures to be seen
outside of Rome. Most of these are

This Etruscan *Chimera*, housed at the Museo
Archeologico, dates from the 5th century BC

displayed on the ground floor and
pride of place is given to the *Chimera*,
part lion, part goat, part snake, cast in
bronze in the 5th century BC. The
bronze was discovered in Arezzo in
1555 and promptly claimed by Cosimo
I. Nearby is the *Arringatore* (Orator),
another fine Etruscan bronze
portraying a member of the Metelli
family and made in the 3rd century BC
when Etruscan aristocrats had already
begun to adopt a Roman lifestyle.

A rich collection of funerary objects
includes a cinerary urn carved in the
form of an Etruscan house and found
near Chiusi. There are also some
outstanding Greek vases and an Egyptian
room containing a very well-preserved
chariot made of wood and bone.

Firenze (Florence)

Via della Colonna 36. Tel: (055) 23575;
www.firenzemusei.it/00_english/
archeologico. Open: Mon 2–7pm, Tue &
Thur 8.30am–7pm, Wed, Fri, Sat & Sun
8.30am–2pm. Admission charge.
Advance booking tel: (055) 294 883.
Nearby: Accademia.

Museo Davanzati

The moment you step into the vestibule of this museum you will receive a vivid impression of the violence of life in 14th-century Florence. Housed in the **Palazzo Davanzati**, this is not simply a palace but a fortress – or even a prison. The four square holes in the ceiling overhead were made to enable the palace occupants to pour boiling pitch or lead on unwelcome guests. The massive inner doors lead into a stone courtyard with a well. Access to the living quarters above is by a narrow, easily guarded staircase.

The palace was built in the mid-14th century and occupied as a family home until 1838. In 1904 it was acquired by an antique dealer, Elia Volpi, who meticulously furnished it as a Florentine home would have appeared in the 14th century.

It was opened as a museum in 1910 and was bought by the state in 1951. Although decidedly dark, the palace is surprisingly comfortable. There is even a serving hatch, moving up through the floors to the kitchen on the upper floor, and two bathrooms.

The Sala Grande (Grand Room) on the first floor is laid out like a drawing room. Next door is the dining room, the Sala dei Pappagalli (Room of the Parrots), so-called because of the parrots which appear on the walls, cleverly painted to resemble tapestries.

The bedroom on the upper floor has an example of a *cassone* – the chest which a Florentine bride received for setting up her household – which is filled with rare linen of the period. The wall painting in this room illustrates a French medieval romance.

The kitchen is on the top floor, as were all kitchens of the period, to reduce the risk of fire. It is fully equipped with antique vessels and other necessary kitchenware.
Palazzo Davanzati, via Porta Rossa 13.
Tel: (055) 238 8610;
www.polomuseale.firenze.it/english/
musei/davanzati. Open: Tue–Sat & 1st
& 3rd Sun in month 8.15am–2pm.
Closed: Mon, 2nd & 4th Sun each
month. Admission charge. Upper floor
closed for restoration.

Museo dell'Opera del Duomo
(Cathedral Works Museum)

Almost every Italian cathedral has transferred some of its more vulnerable treasures to a museum, but Florence has carried this to extremes. Heavy pollution perhaps justifies stripping the exterior of the Baptistery and the Campanile – but much has been removed from the interior of the cathedral as well.

This is the museum you must visit if you want to see the original panels made by Ghiberti for the Baptistery East Doors; six of the panels are on display as they are restored (currently six of the ten panels are on view). You can also see the sculptured panels that originally decorated the lower stages of the Campanile, admittedly much easier to study here at eye level than high up in their original position.

Particularly interesting are the statues which Arnolfo di Cambio made for the planned façade of the cathedral which was never built. There is also a small exhibit illustrating the construction of the dome, together with Brunelleschi's death mask.

Donatello's sculptures from the Campanile are here, together with his choir loft from the cathedral. Michelangelo's agonised *Pietà* (the Virgin holding the body of Christ) is kept here. The bearded figure of Nicodemus, who assists the Virgin, is said to be Michelangelo's self-portrait.

The museum will soon be expanding into the adjoining building, formerly the Teatro degli Intrepedi.
Piazza del Duomo 9.
Tel: (055) 230 2885;
www.operaduomo.firenze.it.
Open: Mon & Thur 9am–11.30pm, Tue, Wed, Fri & Sat 9am–7.30pm, Sun 9am–1.40pm. Admission charge.

Museo di Firenze Com'era (Museum of Florence As It Was)

This museum is mainly devoted to plans, maps, topographical drawings and paintings of Florence. It traces the physical development of the city from the 15th century onwards. One outstanding exhibit is the immense reproduction of the so-called Pianta della Catena (Chain Map) of 1470, the original of which is in Germany. This is not a map as such but a meticulous bird's-eye view of Florence, probably painted from the viewpoint of Bellosguardo, the hill just to the south of the city. A photograph taken from the same viewpoint today would show an astonishing degree of similarity.
Via dell'Oriuolo 24. Tel: (055) 261 6545.
Open: Mon–Wed, Sat 9am–7pm. Closed: Wed in summer. Admission charge.

Museo Nazionale Alinari della Fotografia

Italy's national photographic museum now has its permanent home in the Leopoldine complex on the Piazza Santa Maria Novella. Seven areas exhibit the history of photography from 1839 to the present day, and displays include images from top photographers, photo albums, stationery and cameras. The displays also offer raised reliefs and Braille, for blind and partially sighted visitors.
Piazza Santa Maria Novella. Tel: (055) 216 310; www.alinarifondazione.it.
Open: Thur–Tue 9.30am–7.30pm (until 11.30pm Sat). Closed Wed.
Admission charge.

Museo di San Marco

San Marco was rebuilt as a convent for Dominican monks in 1437, funded by

Cosimo de' Medici and designed by his favourite architect, Michelozzo. It was also equipped with the first public library in Europe.

Today, San Marco is virtually a display case for the frescoes of Fra Angelico, who was a friar here from 1436 to 1455, and, with the help of various assistants, painted devotional scenes on the 44 cells of the dormitory.

Fra Angelico's luminous, gentle works bridge the gap between the Middle Ages and the Renaissance.

Unforgettable is the *Annunciation* which greets the visitor at the top of the steps leading into the dormitory quarters. In this painting, Fra Angelico shows the stunned expression of a young woman who has just been told that she is to be the mother of God.
Piazza San Marco 1.
Tel: (055) 238 8608;
www.firenzemusei.it/00_english/
sanmarco. Open: Mon–Fri
8.15am–1.50pm, Sat 8.15am–6.50pm,
Sun & holidays 8.15am–7pm.
Closed: 1st, 3rd, 5th Sun and 2nd,
4th Mon. Admission charge.
Advance booking tel: (055) 294 883.

Museo Nazionale del Bargello (National Museum of the Bargello)

Few buildings sum up Florence's embattled past so well as this grim fortress in the heart of the city. Begun in 1255, the Bargello served as the city's first town hall. Later it was used as a law court and then, in 1574, it became the headquarters of the Chief of Police.

SAVONAROLA

San Marco became the headquarters of the fanatical monk, Girolamo Savonarola. His portrait hangs in his cell at the end of the dormitory corridor: an ugly, forceful, intelligent face, with a great beak of a nose and burning eyes. Born in 1452, Savonarola came to the monastery in 1489, gaining a reputation for his fiery sermons on cleansing Florence of its sins. He attacked the powerful, corrupt Borgia pope, Alexander V.

In 1494 the Florentines were disgusted with the cowardice of Piero de' Medici, who did not resist the French invasion of the city. Savonarola became virtual ruler of the new Florentine Republic. Under his fanatical regime, at first the Florentines built 'Bonfires of the Vanities' on which priceless works of art and luxuries were burned, but finally they abandoned Savonarola to his enemies. In 1498, he and two companions were hanged and burnt in the Piazza della Signoria.

The portraits of convicted criminals were displayed here and sometimes their bodies as well, following their public execution in the courtyard.

The Bargello continued as a prison until 1859 but became a museum in 1865 and now houses one of Italy's most important collections of sculpture. It is advisable to allow at least two hours to view the collection.

Despite the Bargello's grim history, the courtyard, with its loggia and grand staircase, is beautiful. The ground floor contains work by Michelangelo (1475–1564), Cellini (1500–71) and other late Renaissance artists. Michelangelo's sculptures include the drunken *Bacchus* (1497), his first freestanding statue, and the noble *Brutus* (1539–40) – the only bust he ever made. Look out for Cellini's exquisite preliminary model for *Perseus* (1545). Beside it are the original panels from the finished statue, now displayed in the Loggia dei Lanzi (*see pp64–5*).

Ascending the grand staircase from the courtyard you reach the loggia, which has been turned into a charming aviary for the bronze birds of Giambologna (1529–1608). The door on the right is the entrance to the immense Salone del Consiglio Generale (General Council Chamber). This was originally the law court and now contains the most important works of the early Renaissance. Outstanding even in this company is the work of Donatello (1386–1466), including his *David* (1430–40), the first freestanding nude

Façade of San Marco

since antiquity, plus a smaller marble *David* (1408). In this room, too, are the trial panels showing *The Sacrifice of Isaac* made by Ghiberti and Brunelleschi in the Baptistery doors competition (*see p33*). Other rooms on this floor contain a priceless ivory collection, and collections of Islamic art and Byzantine jewellery. The floor above houses a stunning display of the ceramic work of the Della Robbia family.
Via del Proconsolo 4.
Tel: (055) 238 8606;
www.firenzemusei.it/00_english/bargello.
Open: daily 8.15am–1.50pm, except alternate Sun & Mon. Admission charge.
Advance booking tel: (055) 294 083.
Nearby: Badia Fiorentina.

Palaces
Palazzo Medici-Riccardi
This was the home of the Medici family for over 100 years. Lorenzo the Magnificent was born here and this is where he reluctantly took over the leadership of the city at the age of 20. Kings and emperors were entertained here. It still discharges an important role, for the building now houses various local government offices, but most of the building is open to the public.

Built between 1444 and 1464 by Michelozzo for Cosimo de' Medici, it is a typical example of Florentine understatement. It is also characteristic of the prudence of the early Medici that the palace, large though it is, is set along the street line like an ordinary house. The exterior has three distinct storeys,

the ground floor being in the 'rusticated' style very popular in Florence. Stone benches, on which petitioners once waited, are still in place.

Much of the interior was changed and enlarged by the Riccardi family who bought the palace in 1659.

An elegant arcaded courtyard leads to a pleasant formal walled garden. A lift will take you up to the gallery, a remarkably vulgar confection which was painted in 1683 by the Neapolitan artist, Luca Giordano. The Riccardi probably intended to compliment the Medici by commissioning these scenes glorifying the later members of the clan.

Far more attractive is the great fresco depicting the *Journey of the Three Magi* which occupies three walls of the chapel (Cappella dei Magi). Painted by Benozzo Gozzoli in 1459, it has a joyous, springtime feel about it. It is also an invaluable historical record because Gozzoli included several members of the Medici family and their contemporaries in the scene.

The immensely long procession, complete with camels, is shown winding its way up a hill in Tuscany. The young king on a white horse in the foreground is an idealised portrait of Lorenzo the Magnificent.

His brother Giuliano, who was later murdered, is depicted just behind the black man in a green tunic, carrying a bow. Alongside the bowman is their grandfather, Cosimo, and next to him their father, Piero.

Gozzoli put himself in the picture as well – just behind the Medici – and ensured his immortality by writing his name in gold letters on his red hat.

Via Cavour 3. Tel: (055) 276 0340; www.palazzo-medici.it.
Open: Thur–Tue 9am–7pm.
Admission charge.
Nearby: San Lorenzo.

Palazzo Pitti

Its aggressive display makes the Palazzo Pitti the least Florentine of all the palaces in the city. Now housing several museums, the Palazzo Pitti was built from 1457 for Luca Pitti who was trying to outdo the Medici. Indeed, the plans of the palace were originally offered to Cosimo de' Medici when he was planning the construction of the Palazzo Medici, but he turned them down as being far too ostentatious.

Ironically, after the Pitti's wealth declined they had to sell the building to Eleonara di Toledo, wife of the Medici duke, Cosimo I, in 1549. Cosimo moved into it in 1550 and from then on it served as the home of all the rulers of Florence until 1828. The Pitti Palace was expanded extensively during the 16th century; one of its main architects was Ammannati, who built the imposing courtyard at the core of the palace looking out to the Giardino di Boboli (Boboli Gardens) behind.

The front of the palace faces on to a bare piazza without shade or seats. The palace, like all Florentine museums, is subject to sudden unannounced

The inner courtyard of the Palazzo Medici-Riccardi

closures. Lacking any guidance through its complex layout, the Pitti is the most unfriendly, and the most expensive, of Florence's museums.

At the same time, it is one of the most important. The Medici collected art objects with an almost manic determination, although, as time went on, with diminishing selectivity. Many of the objects they collected remain in the palace, which is divided into no fewer than six museums and art galleries. The picture collection housed in the Galleria Palatina (Palatine Gallery) is second in importance only to the Uffizi. The palace has, however, been deliberately left as a family home. Church services are still held in the Palatine Chapel in the great courtyard and the paintings in the palace itself are displayed exactly as they were originally hung. The opulent rooms are exhibits in their own right and the overall effect is rich but confusing. Altogether, it is advisable to allow several hours for a visit. Some combined tickets are available.

The **Galleria Palatina** is the palace's main display area, access to which is up the vast ceremonial staircase designed by Ammannati. Although there are at least 26 rooms in the Palatine Gallery, the most important paintings are displayed in the five great state rooms which overlook the Piazza del Pitti. The ceiling of each room is decorated with

The fortress-like Pitti Palace seen from the Boboli Gardens

frescoes whose classical subjects have given their names to the rooms: the Sala di Venere (Venus Room) and the Sala di Apollo both have paintings by Titian; the Sala di Marte (Mars) has works by Rubens and Tintoretto; the Sala di Giove (Jupiter) and the Sala di Saturna (Saturn) both have superb works by Raphael. The Sala di Giove also served as the Medici throne room. The Sala dell'Iliade was painted as late as the 19th century with subjects from Homer's epic poem.

The **Galleria d'Arte Moderna** consists mostly of 19th-century paintings, in spite of its name. There are some lively historic battle scenes, and some highly evocative paintings of Tuscan rural life from the early decades of the 20th century.

The **Museo degli Argenti** (Silverware Museum) is on the ground floor (access from the courtyard) and has a far greater range of exhibits than its name implies. Among the many objects on display are the wonderful antique vases collected by Lorenzo the Magnificent, who simply could not resist having his name engraved on them.

Situated in a pavilion in the southern wing of the palace (entered from the Boboli Gardens) is the **Galleria del Costume**, used for changing displays of court and theatrical costume dating from the 18th century up to the 1930s.

Piazza dei Pitti. www.palazzopitti.it. Galleria Palatina, tel: (055) 238 8614. Museo degli Argenti, tel: (055) 238 8709.

Galleria d'Arte Moderna, tel: (055) 238 8616. Galleria del Costume, tel: (055) 238 8713. Galleria Palatina: open Tue–Sun 8.15am–6.50pm, closed Mon. Museo degli Argenti: open daily 8.15am–6.50pm, closed 1st, 3rd, 5th Mon & 2nd, 4th Sun. Galleria del Costume & d'Arte Moderna: open daily 8.15am–1.50pm. Closed: 1st, 3rd, 5th Mon & 2nd, 4th Sun. Admission charges. Advance booking tel: (055) 294 883. Nearby: Boboli Gardens.

Palazzo Strozzi

Although work started on this palace in 1489, only 45 years after the Medici-Riccardi Palace, it nevertheless belongs to a different era. Unlike the reticent Medici-Riccardi Palace, the Strozzi Palace is brutally domineering. Its purpose was to display the power of Filippo Strozzi, the great banker whose wealth rivalled even that of the Medici. For over 15 years Strozzi stealthily bought up property in the city centre, eventually acquiring 15 houses which were demolished to make way for this monster. Building work went on for over 46 years, long after Strozzi's death in 1491. A permanent exhibition on the ground floor illustrates the development of the palace, which is today used for exhibitions, trade fairs and conferences.

Piazza Strozzi. Tel: (055) 277 6461; www.palazzostrozzi.org. Open: during exhibitions only, otherwise visible from exterior. Admission charge for exhibitions.

Palazzo Vecchio
(Old Palace)

This grim but imposing building has been the seat of Florentine government for nearly 700 years, from around 1300 when the palace was finished to the present. The bellowing of the great bell, called *la Vacca* (the Cow), which hung in the soaring, majestic tower, once summoned the citizens at times of danger. Although this building is still the town hall, much of the day-to-day business of local government has been transferred to modern buildings on the outskirts of the city.

The entrance courtyard was designed by Michelozzo in 1453. Cosimo I's court architect, Giorgio Vasari, added the stucco columns and the charming frescoes depicting Austrian cities to welcome Joanna of Austria, the bride of

The Palazzo Vecchio

Cosimo's eldest son, Francesco. The enchanting little fountain of a laughing child holding a dolphin is a 16th-century copy of Verrocchio's *Puttino*. The original can be seen in one of the rooms upstairs.

Beyond the entrance courtyard, stairs to the right lead up to the monumental State Apartments. The first of these is the Salone dei Cinquecento (the Room of the Five Hundred). Here the republican Consiglio Maggiore (Great Council) used to meet after the expulsion of the Medici. Michelangelo and Leonardo da Vinci were both commissioned to decorate it, but neither got beyond the preliminary stages. The room was used as the Italian Parliament for the brief period when Florence was the capital of Italy (1865–70). The present frescoes, the work of Vasari, exalt the military triumphs of Cosimo I. Particularly interesting is the *Siege of Florence*, which shows what Florence looked like in the mid-16th century.

Just off this large room is the smaller Studiolo di Francesco I. Vasari designed this rather claustrophobic study for the scholarly, introverted eldest son of Cosimo I. Francesco was very interested in alchemy and the natural sciences: the decorations reflect these interests. The crowded pictures and statues – among them portraits of Francesco's parents, painted by Bronzino – form a miniature gallery of Florentine Mannerist art.

Next comes the Quartiere di Leone X. Leo X was the first Medici pope, and the decoration of this series of rooms, by Vasari and Bronzino, is unabashed propaganda for the family. Of the remaining rooms, the Sala dei Gigli (Room of the Lilies) is the most splendid. The lily (or *fleur-de-lis*), one of the symbols of Florence, appears all over the walls of this room. Donatello's statue of *Judith and Holofernes*, now

restored, is also displayed here (originally it was ouside in the Piazza della Signora); the statue was made as a warning to tyrants, as the carvings on its base indicate.

Just off this room is the Cancelleria, the office used by Niccolò Machiavelli during his period of office as Secretary to the Republic. It contains his 16th-century bust. Another room that is occasionally open is the notorious L'Alberghetto, 'the little hotel'. This room in the tower was used as a prison. Cosimo de' Medici and Savonarola were both imprisoned here.

Piazza della Signoria. Tel: (055) 276 8224. By reservation, expert guides take groups of 8–10 people to areas of the Palazzo normally not open to the public; these include secret passageways and the roof beams of the Salone dei Cinquecento.

Open: Fri–Wed 9am–7pm, Thur 9am–2pm, some extended hours in summer. Admission charge. Nearby: Uffizi.

The beautiful entrance courtyard with its cherub and dolphin fountain

Piazza della Signoria

For all their artistic genius, the Florentines never learned how to build a decent public square. With the exception of the Piazza Santissima Annunziata, the city's main squares are unremarkable. The cathedral is crowded into the small and shapeless Piazza del Duomo; the Piazza del Pitti is a dreary asphalt waste, and the Piazza della Signoria was never planned. This last square stands at the very heart of the city. Excavations carried out in the 1980s revealed extensive Roman and Etruscan remains beneath the square, and the Palazzo Vecchio partly stands on the site of the Roman theatre.

The citizens of Florence assembled in this square when summoned by the great bell of the Palazzo Vecchio. The square was thus their parliament. Here, too, they welcomed important visitors and punished political enemies (a tablet set approximately in the centre of the piazza marks the site of the execution of Savonarola). Despite this importance, the piazza has no particular shape, unlike the majestic harmony of Siena's main square, the Campo. In fact, the square consists of nothing but a haphazard collection of buildings. It has been like that for over 400 years; a contemporary painting of the execution of Savonarola, which took place in the piazza in 1498, shows it looking almost exactly as it does today. Cosimo I commissioned Michelangelo to build a loggia all the way round to provide a degree of unity,

Ammannati's dramatic *Neptune* fountain, nicknamed 'Big Whitey'

but he never got down to the job. Florentines today like it just the way it is.

Fronting the Palazzo Vecchio is the *arringhiera*, the platform from which members of the city council once addressed the citizens. To the right is a copy of Michelangelo's *David*, a copy of Donatello's *Judith and Holofernes*, and a copy of the same sculptor's *Il Marzocco*, the heraldic lion of the city.

A short step away from these monumental sculptures is the Loggia dei Lanzi, so-called because the German lancers who formed the bodyguard of Cosimo I had their barracks near here. The loggia was built between 1376 and 1382 and forms a graceful porch, even though (whether by accident or design) nearly all the statues placed here depict violent action.

Predominant among them is Cellini's *Perseus;* one of the finest of late Renaissance sculptures (1545), it is also one of the most heartless. Cellini portrays Medusa not as a monster but as a beautiful naked woman – which makes it all the more shocking to see black blood pouring from her severed trunk while Perseus, a handsome youth, complacently holds up the severed head. In his autobiography Cellini describes how he ran out of metal while casting the statue and frantically threw in all the household pewter.

Also in the loggia is Giambologna's *Rape of the Sabines* (1583) and his *Hercules and the Centaur* (1599), together with Pio Fedi's continuance of the tradition into the 19th century, the *Rape of Polyxena* (1866).

To the left of the Palazzo Vecchio's façade is the Neptune Fountain, an enormous, and frequently dry, monster, by Ammannati (1565–75). It had barely been completed before it was nicknamed *Il Biancone* (Big Whitey) and a mocking verse circulated describing how Ammannati had wasted so much good stone.

Further out in the square is the equestrian statue of Duke Cosimo I.

Giambologna worked at this symbol of ducal power for over seven years, from 1587 to 1594. The panels in the pedestal show Cosimo's conquest of Siena (1555) and Pope Pius V bestowing the title of Grand Duke of Tuscany upon him in 1569.

Cellini's *Perseus* holds aloft the severed head of his Medusa

Ponte Santa Trinità

The fact that the Arno runs from east to west through Florence condemned its beautiful bridges towards the end of World War II. The Germans used the river as a defensive line during their northward retreat and all the city's bridges, with the exception of the Ponte Vecchio, were blown up. All these bridges have since been rebuilt exactly as they were before 1944.

Ponte Santa Trinità is the most important of the bridges of Florence both in terms of its siting and because it was deliberately designed as a work of art. The bridge was built (or rather rebuilt, since a bridge had stood here since 1252) on the orders of Cosimo I. The design is attributed to Michelangelo, who is said to have sketched out the subtle, elliptical curve of the arches. Ammannati carried out the actual construction work between 1567 and 1569. Cosimo I did not simply want a bridge across the river linking the two halves of his city, he demanded that the land be raised on both embankments to provide a grand sweeping approach. After the bridge was blown up in 1944 there was a great deal of debate about how the bridge was to be rebuilt. There was even a suggestion that it should be cast in ferro-concrete, but eventually the decision was taken to copy the original plans exactly. Demolished blocks of stone were salvaged from the bed of the river; the quarry in the Boboli Gardens which had supplied the original stone

THE FLOOD OF 1966

The Florentines have little love for their river; Dante referred to it as 'the accursed ditch'. For much of the year the Arno lies low in its channel – but the height of the embankments shows only too clearly how high the river can rise. There had been at least four major floods before the disaster of November 1966. Although there was ample warning, the moment when the banks finally broke occurred with such suddenness that all the people in the railway underpass, some distance from the river, were drowned. Thirty-five people died, and untold numbers of works of art were damaged.

was reworked to supply any blocks that were missing. When the bridge was reopened in 1957 it was complete – all except for the head of Spring, one of the statues of the *Four Seasons* which decorate the two ends of the bridge. The head was finally found in the river in 1961 and ceremonially displayed on a velvet cushion in the Palazzo Vecchio before it was finally rejoined to the body.

Ponte Vecchio (Old Bridge)

The oldest of all Florence's bridges was spared destruction in 1944 because of the intervention of the wartime German consul, Gerhard Wolf. Spanning the narrowest section of the river, this bridge almost certainly stands on the site of the first Roman bridge. The Ponte Vecchio was built in 1345 to replace an earlier wooden bridge that had been washed away by one of the savage floods to which the Arno is subject. It is one of the last surviving bridges in Europe with houses and shops built along it.

Tanners were the first to build workshops on the bridge, using the river to soak their hides. Butchers and blacksmiths also had premises on the bridge but they were all evicted in 1593 on the orders of Ferdinando I, who objected to the smell, noise and mess made by these trades. Goldsmiths then took over the cramped workshops, and they have been there ever since. Today, the Ponte Vecchio is the most popular tourist spot in the city.

Spedale degli Innocenti (Foundling Hospital)

Founded in 1419, this was Europe's first orphanage and it still operates as such, hence the name (O)spedale degli Innocenti. Brunelleschi was commissioned to build the hospital, and the delicate colonnade fronting the orphanage was completed in 1426. The beautiful ceramic plaques (1487) of swaddled babies, set in the spandrels, are the work of Andrea della Robbia. The gallery inside the orphanage (part of the Museo degli Innocenti, or MUDI) contains a number of fine Renaissance paintings, including Ghirlandaio's splendid *Adoration of the Magi*.

Piazza della Santissima Annunziata 12. Tel: (055) 20371; www.istitutodeglinnocenti.it. Open: Mon–Sat 8.30am–7pm, Sun 8.30am–2pm. Admission charge. Nearby: Museo Archeologico.

Ponte Vecchio is Florence's oldest bridge

Three great artists

Leonardo da Vinci (1452–1519)

Leonardo was born in the village of Vinci, the illegitimate son of a Florentine lawyer. His career as a painter serves as a link between the age of the old-fashioned *bottega* (workshop), when the artist was regarded simply as a craftsman, and the High Renaissance, when the artist was courted by princes. One of the paintings on which he worked as a *bottega* apprentice is Verrocchio's *Baptism of Christ*, now hung in room 15 of the Uffizi (*see p51*). Leonardo had a highly analytical mind; in the modern world, perhaps, he might have been a great scientist or engineer. His notebooks are crammed with ideas for new machines, including a helicopter and a tank. Painting was only one of his skills, and many paintings were left unfinished as his mind leapt on to another subject. He died in France where he had been staying as the guest of the king, François I.

Michelangelo Buonarroti (1475–1564)

Michelangelo also trained in a *bottega*, serving very briefly as an apprentice in Ghirlandaio's workshop. At an early age he benefited from Medici patronage for, at the age of 13, he entered the school of art set up by Lorenzo de' Medici. His greatest work of art is in Rome where, under pressure from Pope Julius II, he painted the ceiling of the Sistine Chapel. Nevertheless, he regarded himself primarily as a sculptor. Unlike Leonardo, he was also involved in politics, a passionate republican who

Statue of Leonardo at the Uffizi

A copy of Michelangelo's *David* sculpture stands in the Piazza della Signoria

fought for the defence of Florence against his Medici patrons during the siege of 1530. During that siege he was put in charge of defensive works and supervised the extension of the city walls to embrace the hill and church of San Miniato (*see p75*).

Benvenuto Cellini (1500–71)

Apart from his exquisite sculptures, Cellini is best known for the remarkable *Autobiography* in which he recounted his swashbuckling life in boastful detail, including his claims to have killed scores of people as a gunner during the 1527 siege of Rome, going about this slaughter safe in the knowledge that the Pope had absolved him beforehand 'for any murders I might commit'. His most famous work is *Perseus* in Florence (*see p65*) but he also created a remarkable gold salt cellar for François I of France. His death approximately coincides with the end of the Italian Renaissance.

Walk: Florence south to north

This walk takes you from the southernmost gate of the city, Porta Romana, to the cathedral, passing through streets lined with little shops and workshops. Don't take the walk at rush hour or with children as there is heavy traffic on the first part of the walk, up to the Via Sant'Agostino junction.

Allow 1 hour.

Begin at the Porta Romana.

1 Porta Romana

Florence lost much of its walls and gates when it became the temporary capital of Italy in the 1860s. The enormous Porta Romana (Rome Gate) still has its vast, 6m (20ft) high doors nearly *in situ*. The gate also served as a barracks and custom post. A 14th-century Florentine, Franco Sachetti, tells the story of how a farmer tried to smuggle through eggs hidden in his trousers. A rival informed the customs officer on duty, who courteously insisted the farmer be seated.
Proceed down Via dei Serragli, past the Giardino Torrigiani, a private park.

2 Via dei Serragli

Along this road are workshops and shops. On the right is the Cinema Goldoni, where a plaque records the place Edward Gordon Craig founded a theatre workshop in 1913.
Turn right at the junction with Via Sant'Agostino. Continue on to Piazza Santo Spirito.

3 Piazza Santo Spirito

The square is pleasantly bohemian, with a market and lots of little cafés and shops. The church of Santo Spirito is the work of Brunelleschi (*see pp46–7*). *Carry on down Via Mazzetta to Piazza San Felice, with its enormous column, and turn left up Via Maggio (if you want to go on to the Boboli Gardens, carry on past the Pitti Palace on the right).*

4 Via Maggio

Via Maggio was once called Via Maggiore (Main Street), which better describes its importance. On both sides are palaces dating from the 15th century onwards. The first on the right (Piazza San Felice 8) is the former home of poets Robert Browning and his wife Elizabeth. *Cross the river using Ponte Santa Trinità (see p66) and continue into Piazza Santa Trinità (see p46). Immediately ahead is Via de'Tornabuoni, with its fashionable shops. Turn right along Via Porta Rossa. Navigate carefully here, for you are in the heart of medieval Florence, with its tangle of narrow streets. Continue past the Palazzo Davanzati with its museum, on the right (see p54) until you reach the Mercato Nuovo, also on the right.*

5 Mercato Nuovo

The Mercato Nuovo is the goal of all visitors because of the small bronze fountain on the southern side called *Il Porcellino* (the Little Boar) which dates from 1612; the snout is 'polished' gold, and it is believed that whoever rubs it and throws a coin into the

fountain will return to Florence. *Continue down Via Porta Rossa and turn left into Via dei Calzaiuoli.*

6 Via dei Calzaiuoli

It is typical of Florence that this lively street, the true 'High Street' of the city, does not have a grand name but is simply called the 'Street of the Hosiers'. Everyone comes here to shop and stroll after work. On summer evenings it is also the haunt of buskers, fortune-tellers, jugglers, musicians and artists. *Continue up the street to reach Piazza del Duomo, with the Baptistery to the left and the Duomo (cathedral) to the right.*

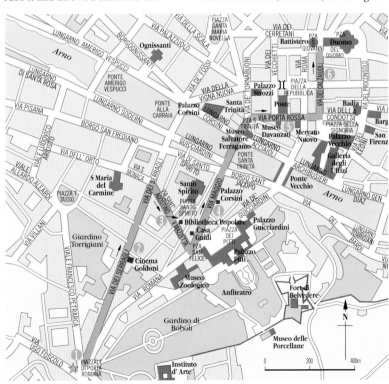

Walk: Florence west to east

This semicircular route covers a number of interesting sights in the north of the city not normally seen by visitors.

Allow 1½ hours.

Begin at the main railway station, Santa Maria Novella.

1 Stazione Centrale di Santa Maria Novella

Fascist Italy built some good railway stations, including this one in 1933. However, the forecourt outside is absurdly designed, and pedestrians and traffic battle for space. Opposite is the great church of Santa Maria Novella (*see pp43 & 46*).

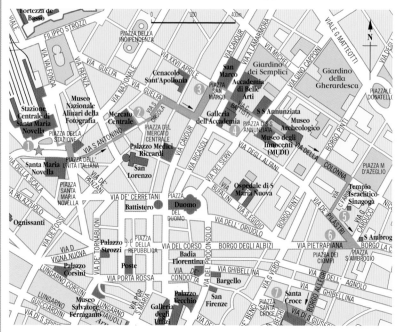

Take the underpass from in front of the station into Piazza dell'Unità Italiana, and from there walk up Via Sant'Antonino, a delightful and lively little street. Take the second left, Via dell'Ariento, full of market stalls on most days. Walk through the stalls and look for the Mercato Centrale on the right.

2 Mercato Centrale

This vast covered food market has numerous cafés, cooked-food stalls and a *tavola calda* canteen, much used by local workers, where you can choose a three-course meal with wine for about €8.

Exit the market by the back doors on to Piazza del Mercato Centrale and head towards Via Rosina. Turn left into Via Taddea and immediately right into Via S Orsola. Turn right again along Via Guelfa, then left along Via Cavour. Continue up to Piazza San Marco.

3 Piazza San Marco

This square stands in the heart of the university district. Ahead is San Marco Convent (*see pp55–6*).

Cross Piazza San Marco, bearing right to exit past the Accademia di Belle Arti, walking down Via C Battisti.

4 Piazza della Santissima Annunziata

This brings you to one of Florence's very few planned Renaissance squares, the beautiful Piazza della Santissima Annunziata, with the splendid colonnade of the Spedale degli

Innocenti to the west (*see p67*).

Exit through the arch alongside the Spedale degli Innocenti which leads into Via della Colonna. The pavements along this street are either narrow or don't exist. At Piazza M d'Azeglio turn right into Via LC Farini to the Tempio Israelitico-Sinagoga (Synagogue).

5 Tempio Israelitico-Sinagoga

A small museum on the first floor of the Synagogue (built 1874–82) illustrates the history of Florentine Jewry (*open: Mon–Thur 11am–1pm & 2–5pm, Fri & Sun 10am–1pm*).

Continue down Via LC Farini, then turn left into Via de'Pilastri to Piazza Sant'Ambrogio. Turn right, down Via Pietrapiana, to reach the Piazza dei Ciompi on the left.

6 Piazza dei Ciompi

The rebellion of the *ciompi*, the lowest level of Florentine cloth workers, against the nobles in the 14th century was an important step towards republicanism. Vasari built the Loggia del Pesce, which stands to one side of the square and is an unusually elegant arcade.

Leave the square by following Borgo Allegri southwards, heading for the enormous bulk of Santa Croce (see pp40–42), then turn right along Via di S Giuseppe to enter Piazza Santa Croce.

7 Piazza Santa Croce

Surrounded by medieval buildings, this is the centre of a living community where local artists display their work.

Walk: Rural Florence

This will take you within a matter of minutes from the hurly-burly of the Ponte Vecchio to the tranquillity of olive groves and gardens. The walk is ideal for children, although they will have to walk up some steep streets and climb some flights of steps.

Allow 2 hours.

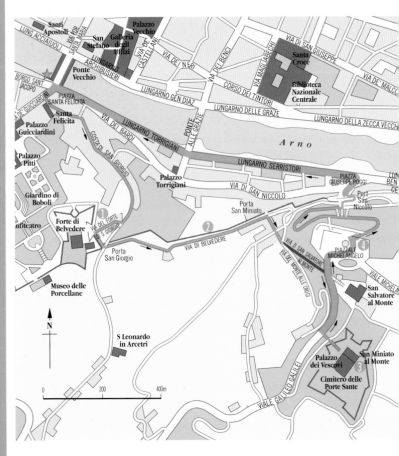

Leave the Ponte Vecchio at its southern end and take the second left into Piazza Santa Felicita. Leave the piazza by the lane to the right of the church façade, the Costa di San Giorgio. About halfway up you will pass No 19, on the right, where Galileo once lived. Turn right at the junction with Via del Forte di San Giorgio for the Forte di Belvedere.

1 Forte di Belvedere

Also known as the Forte di San Giorgio, this huge fortress was built by the Medici from 1590 to 1595 – not to protect the citizens but to overawe them. The gun ports point towards the city! The fortress provides a superb vantage point from which to view Florence. *On leaving the fort, turn immediately right and then left at the junction into the Via di Belvedere.*

2 Via di Belvedere

This well-named lane (literally 'Good View Road') runs along the foot of the mighty city wall, built in the 13th century and heightened in the 16th century. To the right you will catch glimpses of olive groves descending steeply into the valley, while high up in the distance is the gleaming marble front of San Miniato al Monte, your ultimate destination. *Descend the steep lane to reach Porta San Miniato. Turn right here towards Via del Monte alle Croci and, after a short climb, look for a steep flight of steps on the left, called Via del San Savatore al Monte. At the top of the steps turn right in the wide*

Viale Galileo Galilei and, after a short distance, cross the road to ascend the flight of steps that leads up to the church of San Miniato al Monte.

3 San Miniato al Monte

Begun in 1013, this is one of the most splendid Romanesque churches in Tuscany. It is also the second oldest in Florence. The dramatic green, black and white marble front of San Miniato was begun in 1090 and paid for by the Arte di Calimala, the wealthy Guild of Cloth Importers (the Guild's emblem, an eagle holding a bale of cloth in its talons, crowns the roof). The solemn, majestic interior is almost entirely unchanged since it was built. The marble pavement, inlaid with the signs of the Zodiac and animals and birds, dates from 1207 (*open: summer 8am–7.30pm, winter 8am–12.30pm & 2.30–7.30pm*).
Retrace your steps along Viale Galileo Galilei, and so enter Piazzale Michelangelo.

4 Piazzale Michelangelo

This elevated square provides the most famous view of Florence.
To return to central Florence, look for a short flight of steps to the left of the piazzale and follow this to a series of footpaths which lead down the hillside. The paths will take you down to the Lungarno Serristori, running alongside the river. Turn left here and a ten-minute walk will take you back to the Ponte Vecchio.

Excursions from Florence

The area around Florence holds many charms for those looking to leave the beaten track and explore beyond the city's boundaries.

Fiesole

High on its hill, about 25 minutes by bus from the city centre, Florence's old enemy is now its playground. Founded by the Etruscans and then developed by the Romans, Fiesole was the first city to be conquered by Florence. Its most popular feature is the great **Roman theatre**. Tucked into the side of the hill, its grass-covered ruins make it a pleasant

Fiesole

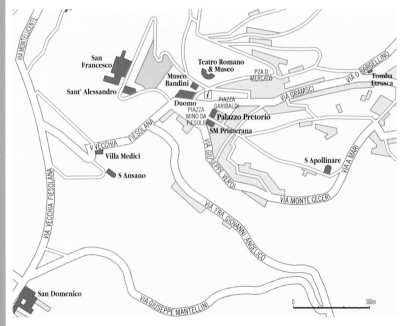

spot for a picnic – and the adjoining museum adds interest. The monastery of San Francesco stands to the west of the main square on the site of an Etruscan temple, and provides superb views.

8km (5 miles) northeast of Florence. Bus 7 from Florence. Tourist Office: Via Portigiani 3. Tel: (055) 598 720; www.comune.fiesole.fi.it. Roman Theatre: Via Portigiani 1. Tel: (055) 59477. Open: winter Wed–Mon 9.30am–5pm; summer daily 9.30am–7pm. Admission charge. Box office tel: (055) 596 1293.

Pistoia

Pistoia is the capital of Tuscany's smallest province and it tends to be overlooked because the historic core is surrounded by ugly industrial suburbs. In compensation is the fact that much of the city within the 14th-century walls is largely unspoiled. The enormous Piazza del Duomo is the heart of the city. Buildings include the 12th-century green-and-white-striped *duomo* (cathedral), the 14th-century Baptistery, and the Palazzo della Podesta of the same date. The late 13th-century Palazzo del Comune houses the **Museo Civico** (city art gallery). The façade of the Ospedale del Ceppo bears a famous terracotta frieze.

37km (23 miles) northwest of Florence. Tourist Information Office: Piazza del Duomo 1. Tel: (0573) 21622; www.pistoia.turismo.toscana.it. Museo Civico: Piazza del Duomo. Tel: (0573) 371 296. Open: Tue &

Thur–Sat 10am–6pm, Wed 4–7pm, Sun 11am–6pm (winter closes one hour earlier). Admission charge. Trains run regularly from Florence.

Prato

A revealing account of life in medieval Italy is Iris Origo's biography *The Merchant of Prato*. Based on the archives of wealthy wool merchant Francesco Datini, it gives us an intimate picture of life in the 14th century. Six hundred years later, cloth is still Prato's major industry.

Inside its girdling walls, the old city remains largely intact. In Piazza del Comune, there is a statue of Datini and the city's art gallery (**Museo Civico**), housed in the Palazzo Pretorio. At the heart of the city is the *duomo* (cathedral), with its pulpit located on the outside wall of the church, carved by Donatello and used to display the miraculous Girdle of the Virgin on ceremonial occasions.

Do not miss the great **Castello dell'Imperatore**, built in the 13th century. Although the castle is empty, its wall walks provide a panorama of the city.

19km (12 miles) northwest of Florence. Tourist Information Office: Via Luigi Muzzi 28. Tel: (0574) 35141; www.prato.turismo.toscana.it. Castello dell'Imperatore: Piazza delle Carceri. Open: Apr–Sept Wed–Mon 9am–1pm, 4–7pm; Oct–Mar Wed–Mon 9am–1pm. Admission charge. Regular trains from Florence. Museo Civico closed for renovations.

Walk: Fiesole to Settignano

This 6km (4-mile) rural walk will take you through woods and open countryside, from one exquisite hilltop town to the next. The first part of the walk is along a narrow, winding main road, so watch out for traffic. Take refreshments with you, as there are no shops or cafés along the route.

Allow 2 hours.

The No 7 bus takes you to Fiesole from central Florence. At the terminus, on Piazza Mino da Fiesole, head eastwards (uphill, away from the cathedral) towards the bronze equestrian statue of Vittorio

Emanuele II meeting Garibaldi (1906) in front of the town hall (Palazzo Pretorio). Then walk leftwards into Piazza Garibaldi, and from there down Via Gramsci, following the signposts to Vincigliata.

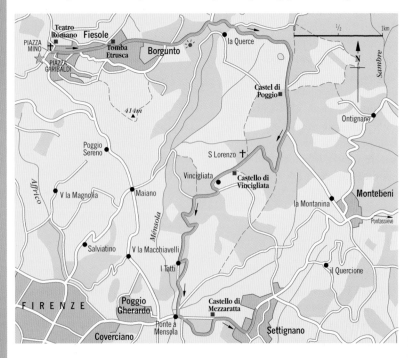

Etruscan tombs

A few hundred metres further along, a sign indicates the existence of Etruscan tombs (*Tomba Etrusca*) down the lane on the left – two massive structures set in a little green garden.

Retrace your steps back to the main road and continue on.

Viewpoint

About 1km (½ mile) further along is a spectacular view back to the Roman amphitheatre at Fiesole, over the olive groves stretching down into the valley.

The road now enters a pine forest. The countryside here is curiously empty for such a densely populated region. It is difficult to believe that, at almost any point, a bus could take you back to Florence within the space of a few minutes. At the next T-junction take the well-signposted road to Settignano/Vincigliata and continue through the wood.

Castles

Little traffic comes down this country road, so you can now relax and enjoy the superb scenery. On the right you can see the Castel di Poggio clinging to an escarpment. At the junction beyond, take the road to Vincigliata. You now enter an open country of vineyards and olive groves. About halfway down the hill is the Castello di Vincigliata, first built in 1031 and sacked by English mercenaries in the 14th century. John Temple Leader, an English Member of Parliament, restored the castle in 1855. On the wall facing the road a series of plaques announces the names of the notables who visited him here, including Princess Beatrice, the daughter of Queen Victoria. The castle is not open to the public.

Continue on down to the bend, turning left to the Villa I Tatti, once the home of world-famous art historian Bernard Berenson (1865–1959) and now a Centre for Italian Renaissance Studies. The road continues to descend gently to Ponte a Mensola.

Ponte a Mensola

This hamlet stands in an idyllic spot with a little river running through it. Look for the two plaques which record the extraordinary number of famous English and American authors who were attracted to this region. Boccaccio spent his childhood here and used a local building, the Villa di Poggio Gherardo, as the setting for some of the early scenes in the *Decameron*.

Turn left and continue uphill to Settignano.

Settignano

This delightful little town still maintains an independent life, despite being so close to Florence, and it is not as overwhelmed by tourists as Fiesole. Desiderio da Settignano (1430–64), the early Renaissance sculptor, grew up here and is commemorated by a statue. The main square has an excellent *gelateria*.

From the main square the No 10 bus will take you back to Florence.

Arezzo

Arezzo is a bustling city with a population of around 90,000. Wartime bombing took its toll on the city, although happily the major monuments escaped, and there has been a considerable amount of modern building to the south. Nevertheless, recent development has been kept outside the city walls, and traffic has now been banned from the centre of what was, until quite recently, one of the most traffic-choked cities in Tuscany.

The copy of the startling *Chimera* statue near the railway station provides a clue to Arezzo's origins. The ancient Etruscan statue, discovered near the city in 1555, dates from the 5th century BC when Arezzo was one of the leaders of the Etruscan federation – the Dodecapolis (the Twelve Cities) – which controlled central Tuscany before Rome flexed its muscles and took over all Italy. It remained an important city during Roman times. Maecenas, wealthy patron of Horace and Virgil, was born here.

In the turbulent Middle Ages, Arezzo was famous – or notorious – for its warrior bishops who ruled the city and led its citizens into many a battle to defend their independence. In the end, like so many cities in Tuscany, it fell under the rule of Florence.

In Arezzo you can see one of the supreme works of the Renaissance: the frescoes of Piero della Francesca. Arezzo was also the birthplace of two key figures, Petrarch and Vasari, and of the monk, Guido d'Arezzo, who invented modern musical notation in the early 11th century.

80km (50 miles) southeast of Florence. Regular trains from Florence. Tourist Information Office, Piazza della Repubblica 28. Tel: (0575) 377 678; www.apt.arezzo.it

Casa di Petrarca (Petrarch's House)

Francesco Petrarca, better known as Petrarch, was born in Arezzo in July 1304 to a Florentine family that had been expelled during one of several political purges that took place in that city (Dante had been sent into exile at the same time).

The house of his birth was originally built in the late 13th century; it was almost completely destroyed by a bombing raid in 1943, and rebuilt in 1948. Today, it is the seat of the scholarly Accademia Petrarca, dedicated to studying the life and times of the man who became renowned all over

Europe as a scholar, poet and humanist. His great sonnet sequence, inspired by his unrequited love for a mysterious woman called Laura, had an enormous influence on other writers, including Shakespeare. The library is used to show manuscripts and published editions of his works as well as innumerable biographies. You can also see interesting historical photographs of Arezzo, including some that show the terrible effects of wartime bombing.
Via dell'Orto 28. Tel: (0575) 24700; www.accademiapetrarca.it.
Open: 10am–noon, 3–5pm.
Closed: Sat afternoon, Sun & bank holidays. Free admission.

Casa di Vasari (Vasari's House)

Giorgio Vasari (1511–74) is often pilloried by art historians because of his sycophantic attitude to the Medici. He was, however, a very good draughtsman, a more-than-adequate architect, and a prolific artist, even if much of his work is serviceable rather than inspired.

Vasari's main claim to fame, however, is the fact that he was the very first art historian, and his book, *Lives of the Most Excellent Painters, Sculptors and Architects*, contains illuminating biographies of the great artists of the Renaissance. On the walls and ceilings in his over-decorated home he painted portraits of the greatest artists of his age.

He also painted a self-portrait in the main room overlooking the street; he shows himself with his back to the observer sitting at a window seat and looking through a window – the same window and window seat you can see in the room today.
Via XX Settembre 55. Tel: (0575) 409 040. Open: Mon, Wed–Sat 9am–7pm, Sun 9am–1pm. Closed: Tue. Admission charge (ring the bell if it is closed).

Duomo (Cathedral)

Arezzo stands on a hill which slopes steadily upwards before coming to an abrupt halt at steep cliffs. The commanding position at the top of the hill – with the city falling away on one side, and open country, with a view towards the mountains, on the other – would seem to be the natural site for a major building.

Considering the great age of the city, therefore, it is curious that no major

A room with a view: giving Vasari's house a thorough airing

Palazetto della Fraternità dei Laici, Piazza Grande

building appeared here until the cathedral was commenced in 1276. Even then, work went ahead only sporadically and it was only completed in 1510.

Even the bell tower, although it looks medieval, is in fact a 19th-century addition, and the façade itself was not completed until the early years of the 20th century.

The interior, though austere, is impressive. The stained-glass windows, a relatively rare art form in Italy, make an immediate impression. These are outstanding in quality and are the work of the 16th-century master, Frenchman Guillaume de Marcillat (William of Marseilles), who also painted the first three vaults of the nave.

In the right-hand aisle is the tomb of Pope Gregory X (1205–76). In the manner of the period, the tomb is a re-used Roman sarcophagus of the 4th century. Gregory died in Arezzo on his way back from France after proclaiming a Crusade.

On the left-hand side of the nave is the most important monument in the cathedral, both from an historical and from an artistic point of view – the tomb of Bishop Guido Tarlati. He was the most warlike of the fighting bishops of Arezzo and he ruled the city from 1312 until his death in 1327, having crushed all internal dissent and led the city successfully in wars against Florence and Siena. The tomb is carved with scenes from the bishop's life but these are set high up on the wall and difficult to see – in order to appreciate the details you will have to buy one of the postcards or guides on sale in the church. Next to the tomb is a beautiful fresco by Piero della Francesca showing Mary Magdalene holding the perfume jar whose contents she used to wipe the feet of Christ.

Piazza del Duomo. Tel: (0575) 23991; www.oparezzo.it. Open: daily 8.30am–12.30pm, 3–6.30pm. Free admission.

Museo Archeologico

Arezzo's excellent Archaeological Museum occupies part of a 16th-century monastery built up against the curving side of the Roman amphitheatre; the windows of the museum look out on to the amphitheatre itself, one of the best preserved in Tuscany (now a public garden entered from Via F Crispi). The museum houses a collection of Etruscan and Roman remains found in and around Arezzo and has a series of rooms devoted to the famous Aretine wares that were made in Arezzo between 50 BC and AD 70, pottery notable for its lively decorative scenes in low relief.

Via Margaritone 10. Tel: (0575) 20882. Open: daily 8.30am–7.30pm. Admission charge.

Museo Diocesano del Duomo

This small museum contains works of art removed from the cathedral. They include frescoes by Arezzo's own artist, Spinello Aretino (Aretino is the name for citizens of Arezzo), and paintings by Giorgio Vasari.

Via San Domenico. www.oparezzo.it. Open: Mon–Sat 9am–noon. Closed: Sun. Free admission.

Museo Statale d'Arte Medioevale e Moderna

Despite its rather grand title (The State Museum of Modern and Medieval Art), this museum is 'local' in the best sense of the word. It is housed in the handsome 15th-century Palazzo Bruni which modestly occupies the corner of two streets. The courtyard is worth looking at in its own right for it is probably the work of Bernardo Rossellino (1409–64). It is used to display a great variety of interesting sculptural fragments brought here from other buildings in the city. Most of the paintings on display within the museum are the work of local artists. Vasari, Arezzo's most successful self-publicist, has an immense work entitled *The Banquet of Esther and Ahasuerus*. Vasari used his wife as the model for Esther.

Via San Lorentino 8. Tel: (0575) 409 050. Open: Tue–Sun 9am–7pm. Closed: Mon. Admission charge.

Piazza Grande

The Piazza Grande starts at the core of the historic city. A new centre of

Arezzo's Piazza Grande, the site of a monthly antiques market

commercial life has now developed further down the hill so that this ancient square is now a charming and tranquil backwater. Most of the shops around the square specialise in antiques and it is here that a large and popular antiques market is held on the first Sunday of every month. It is also the setting for the Giostra del Saracino (Joust of the Saracen) festival, held throughout the summer (*see p21*).

Pieve di Santa Maria

The distinctive bell tower of Santa Maria is known as 'the tower of a hundred holes' because of its many openings. The façade, though weathered, is a splendid example of Romanesque decorative work. Inside, this grand Romanesque church, built at the turn of the 13th century, is solemn and austere.

Most of the ornamentation is in the form of carving, but there is a polyptych by Pietro Lorenzetti in the choir.
Corso Italia. Tel: (0575) 22629; www. santamariadellapieve.it. Open: daily 9am–1pm, 3–6pm. Free admission.

San Francesco

Built in the early 14th century and never completed, this vast barn of a church contains one of the most compelling of all Renaissance fresco cycles, the *Legend of the True Cross* by Piero della Francesca (1420–92). This immense work occupies the whole of the sanctuary behind the high altar and

PIERO DELLA FRANCESCA

Piero della Francesca (1420–92) is known as a great early Renaissance artist on the strength of a handful of frescoes. You can see his *Legend of the True Cross* in Arezzo, but to see what art historians call 'the greatest picture in the world' you must visit the Museo Civico in the Palazzo Comunale, in the little town of Sansepolcro, 39km (24 miles) northeast of Arezzo. Visitors queue up to view della Francesca's *Resurrection* fresco which, like all his other work, has a mysterious, dream-like quality unlike any other art of the time. Art historian Kenneth Clark, who wrote the definitive account of della Francesca's work, says the fresco expresses 'values for which no rational statement is adequate'. Equally awe-inspiring is the artist's *Madonna del Parto* (Pregnant Madonna) fresco in the tiny hilltop town of Monterchi, midway between Arezzo and Sansepolcro.

it traces the history of the wood of the Cross from the tree planted by Adam down to the rediscovery of the buried Cross by St Helena, mother of Emperor Constantine the Great.
Piazza San Francesco. Open: daily 8.30am–noon & 2–6.30pm. Free admission. Advance booking required to view Legend of the True Cross (*tel: (0575) 352 727; www.pierodellafrancesca.it*).

AREZZO'S ETRUSCAN NEIGHBOURS

Chiusi and Cortona are both delightful little cities that will extend your knowledge of the ancient Etruscans. Both cities can be reached by train from Arezzo; the station for Cortona is at Camucia, 5km (3 miles) away, but with a regular bus service between the station and Cortona. There is also a regular bus service between Arezzo and Cortona.

Chiusi

This ancient city was known to the Etruscans as Camars and its king was the famous Lars Porsena who laid siege to Rome in 510 BC. Underneath the medieval city lies an immense necropolis, and some of the ancient Etruscan tombs have wall paintings. Guided tours can be arranged at the **Archaeological Museum** which also contains a number of Etruscan artefacts, including carved sarcophagi. *Archaeological Museum, Via Porsenna. tel: (0578) 20177. Open: Mon–Sat 9am–2pm, Sun 9am–1pm. Admission charge.*

Cortona

This enchanting little hilltop town, which seems to float high above the Val di Chiana plain, is even older than Chiusi: legend claims that it was founded by Dardanus, who later founded Troy. Impossible to prove, this nevertheless ties in with the theory that the Etruscans came from Asia Minor. Situated at over 600m (1,968ft) above sea level, the city is virtually one vast fortress with its steep, narrow streets and superb vistas.

The **Museo dell'Accademia Etrusca** occupies a 13th-century palace and contains medieval and Renaissance artefacts as well as many important

Etruscan finds. The **Museo Diocesano** in the Piazza del Duomo contains works by Cortona's most important Renaissance artist, Luca Signorelli (1441–1523), but the star of the collection is Fra Angelico's delicate *Annunciation* altarpiece.

Tourist office: Via Nazionale 42.
Tel: (0575) 630 352; www.apt.arezzo.it.
Museo dell'Accademia Etrusca: Piazza Signorelli 9. Tel: (0575) 630 415;
www.accademia-etrusca.org.
Open: May–Sept Tue–Sun 10am–7pm;
Oct–Apr Tue–Sun 10am–5pm.
Closed: Mon. Admission charge.
Museo Diocesano: Piazza del Duomo 1.
Tel: (0575) 62830. Open: May–Sept Tue–Sun 10am–7pm; Oct–Apr Tue–Sun 10am–5pm. Closed: Mon. Admission charge.

The hilltop town of Cortona

Walk: Arezzo town

This walk will take you right through the heart of the historic city.

Allow 1 hour.

Begin at the railway station forecourt.

1 Stazione

The station marks the division between the historic city on its hill (population around 14,000) and the modern city on the plain outside the walls (population 80,000). Look for the Chimera Fountain on the right, on the other side of Via Spinello. This is an excellent copy of the ancient Etruscan statue found near Arezzo in 1555 (the original can be seen in Florence, *see p53*).

2 Via Guido Monaco

Opposite the station is the start of the modern Via Guido Monaco, a handsome avenue crowned by the battlement tower of the medieval Palazzo Municipale. The road is named after Guido d'Arezzo, a monk (*monaco*): about the year 1020, he invented the system of musical notation on which all modern music is based. His statue stands in the little tree-shaded piazza, halfway up the avenue.
Walk all the way up Via Guido Monaco and turn right at the top into Piazza San Francesco.

3 San Francesco

On the right is the immense church of San Francesco, which contains the Renaissance fresco of Piero della Francesca (*see p84*).
Turn right out of the church, and walk along Via Cavour, then turn left up Corso Italia. Turn right past Pieve di Santa Maria with its striking campanile (see p84). This will bring you into the Piazza Grande. Cross the piazza heading for the left-hand corner and ascend the flight of steps up to the Passeggiata del Prato.

4 Passeggiata del Prato

The Passeggiata, a public park, is a green, quiet, tree-shaded spot, ideal for a restful hour or so.
Cross the Passeggiata to the right to the Fortezza Medicea.

5 Fortezza Medicea

A long, grim tunnel will take you up to the centre of the fortress which forms an extension of the park. Follow the rampart round for a view of the

relatively unspoiled valley of the Casentino. Not far up that valley the Battle of Campaldino was fought between Florence and Arezzo in 1289. The poet Dante Alighieri took part in the battle. Though Florence won, so many citizen-soldiers died on both sides that, thereafter, most Italian cities hired foreign mercenaries to fight on their behalf (*see pp100–101*).
Return to the Passeggiata and walk to the far side, to the east end of the Duomo (cathedral). From the flight of steps there is an excellent view to the right of the city wall. The open space alongside the wall is

now used as a market garden. Turn left, then right into Via San Domenico, then left down Via XX Settembre.

6 Casa di Vasari

On the right of this street, part way down, is the home of one of Arezzo's most famous citizens (*see p81*).
The steeply descending street will take you down to the Piaggia del Murello. Turn left and climb up past the Duomo (see pp81–2) to return to the Piazza Grande. Here you can enjoy a drink at one of the open-air restaurants in the Loggia Vasari, located on the north side of the square.

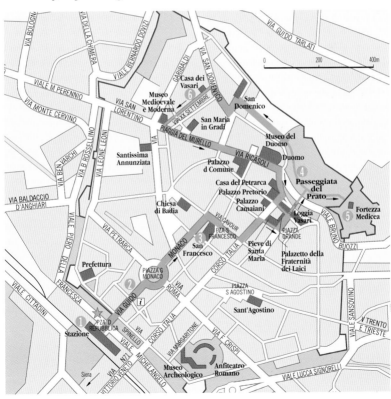

Carrara

Remarkably, Carrara has maintained its identity over many centuries. It is the marble capital of the world; its very name derives from the ancient Etruscan word kar, *meaning 'stone'. The Romans came here for top-quality marble, as did Michelangelo. Half a million tonnes are exported annually, and Carrara has expanded enormously since World War II. The entire area between the old city and the resort of Marina di Carrara, on the coast 4km (2½ miles) away, is now a solid mass of buildings.*

Drive up the endless Viale XX Settembre bisecting this sprawl, to enter the old city. Towering around it are the sharp white peaks of the Apuan Alps, looking snowcapped even in summer; in fact, it's the gleaming white marble of Carrara. A milk-white mountain stream runs through the city's centre, and small marble-processing workshops use its waters to keep cutting equipment cool.
126km (78 miles) northwest of Florence and 55km (34 miles) north of Pisa. Carrara is on the main coastal railway line from Pisa. The station is at Carrara Avenza, 3km (2 miles) from the city centre. There are frequent bus connections from the bus terminal on Piazza Matteotti. Tourist Information Office: Viale XX Settembre. Tel: (0585) 844 136; www.aptmassacarrara.it

Accademia di Belle Arti (School of Fine Arts)

The Accademia is located in one of the grim fortresses which stud the area. The courtyard, open to the public, has displays of ancient Roman sculptures.
Piazza Accademia. Tel: (0585) 71658; www.accademiacarrara.it

Duomo (Cathedral)

This is Carrara's principal monument. It is a child of the mountains: the marble used to build it was quarried just up the road. The west front of this Romanesque, 11th-century building is particularly impressive, with a superb rose window inserted in the 14th century. Inside you will see 14th- and 15th-century sculptures in marble and wood. Nearby, a plaque identifies the house where Michelangelo stayed while working in the quarries.
Piazza del Duomo. Open: daily 8am–1pm & 3.30–6pm. Closed: during religious services. Check with Carrara tourist office. Free admission.

Carrara town

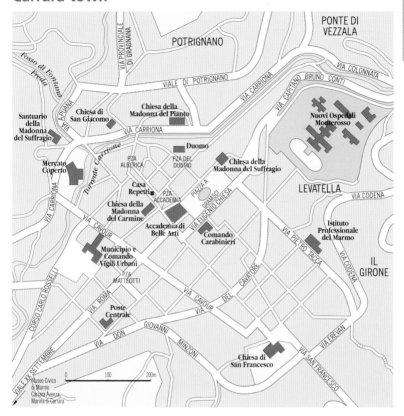

Museo Civico di Marmo (City Marble Museum)

From Piazza Matteotti, buses run to this museum, located on the right-hand side of the Viale XX Settembre going towards the coast, and 2km (1 mile) from the city centre. The museum tells the story of how marble is produced and used.

Viale XX Settembre. Tel: (0585) 845 746. Open: May–Sept 10am–6pm, July & Aug until 8pm. Oct–Apr 9am–5pm. Closed: Sun. Admission charge.

Piazza Alberica

This café-lined street is the social heart of Carrara. Although there is no building of outstanding importance here, the 16th-century palaces which surround the piazza collectively make up a superb townscape.

Piazza Gramsci

The main feature of this square is an extraordinary fountain – a large marble sphere turned round by tiny jets of water.

Quarries

The Emperor Augustus boasted that he found Rome built in brick, and left it in marble. All over Italy other cities followed suit, cladding their important buildings in the same beautiful, polished, gleaming stone. Much of that marble came from Carrara; sculptors in particular used the flawless stone for their major works.

The quarries fell into decline in the early Middle Ages but received a tremendous boost during the Renaissance. Michelangelo was a familiar figure here in the 16th century, spending days clambering around the quarries looking for the perfect stone for his work. In one of his letters he recounts the difficulties involved in moving the huge blocks of marble intended for St Peter's. He also made the point that the Florentine stone-workers he brought with him were of little use, being unskilled in the handling of marble. Even today, the Carrarese marble-workers have a skill that few can equal.

Despite the millions of tonnes of marble that have been extracted from

Slabs of Carrara marble

A Carrara marble quarry

of metres in length, which moves slowly forward on pulleys. A typical Carrara quarry presents an unforgettable sight: blindingly white against the blue sky, the blocks and steps of marble look like titanic buildings or sculptures.

To visit one of the quarries of Carrara, take the old road signposted to Colonnata that leads eastward from Carrara city centre into the mountains. Once you reach Colonnata, 8km (5 miles) from the city centre, you will see plenty of signs saying Cave di Marmo, indicating a quarry.

the hills around Carrara, millions more remain. Quarrying began in Roman times and still goes on, making this one of the world's oldest industrial sites in continuous use. The Romans extracted the marble by hammering pegs of figwood into natural fissures, then pouring water over them so that they expanded and cracked the stone. In the 19th century gunpowder was used, with harmful effects on the stone – as shown by the deterioration of the façade of Florence Cathedral. Today, the stone is cut with a continuous wire band saw, hundreds

Statues and sculptures in a marble worker's workshop

Lucca

Even in a country where the preservation of historic city centres is regarded as the norm, rather than a cause to be fought for, Lucca stands out. It is a large city, with a population of around 93,000 (in the same league as Pisa), but most of the people live in the suburbs. This leaves the historic centre, shielded by its enormous walls, an unspoiled gem of a Tuscan city.

Lucca is Roman in origin: Caesar, Pompey and Crassus met here to form the First Triumvirate. One of the city's most intriguing sights is the Roman amphitheatre. The city also has an unusually high number of good medieval and Renaissance palaces and more than its fair share of impressive Romanesque churches.

Unlike other characterful Tuscan cities, such as Montepulciano, Lucca is by no means off the beaten track. On the contrary, its near neighbours are the booming industrial cities of Pisa and Pistoia. A major international airport lies almost at its doorstep and it is on a main railway line. The city is therefore fully in touch with the 21st century. Its citizens are among the most prosperous in Italy, drawing their wealth partly from the soil (the province of Lucca produces some of Italy's best olive oil) and from small family firms in the city itself.

Lucca, however, has learned to take only the best of modern developments.

Long before many other European cities realised the destructive effects of heavy traffic, the Lucchesi set about barring it from the area within the city walls. Some could argue that this was far less of a hardship than it might have been, because Lucca is totally flat and quite unlike the steep, hilly towns of central Tuscany. The Lucchese have thus adopted cycling as their preferred form of transport and within the city walls the bicycle is used by young and old alike (visitors can hire bicycles at the tourist office in Piazzale G Verdi).

74km (46 miles) west of Florence, 22km (14 miles) northeast of Pisa. Lucca is on the main railway line connecting Viareggio–Florence via Pisa, and there is a regular bus service from both Florence and Pisa.
Regional Tourist Information Office: Piazza Santa Maria 35. Tel: (0583) 919 931. Municipal Tourist Office: Piazzale Verdi. Tel: (0583) 442 944; www.luccatourist.it

Anfiteatro Romano (Roman Amphitheatre)

Lucca's main street is the Via Fillungo and this lives up to its name (which means 'long thread') by being little more than a narrow lane winding its way between high buildings. Just off its northern section is the Roman amphitheatre. There are many Roman amphitheatres in Italy but none so odd as this. The amphitheatre itself has gone, but its shape is perfectly preserved like a fossil by the houses that were built up against its outer wall. These houses now form an elliptical circuit and the four entrances into the piazza occupy the same position as the original four gates into the amphitheatre.

Casa Natale di Puccini (Puccini's Birthplace)

The birthplace of Giacomo Puccini (1858–1924) has been set out as a shrine to one of Italy's most popular operatic composers. Quite apart from its association with Puccini, the building is of interest in itself as a good example of a 15th-century town house. The objects on display range from the Steinway grand piano on which Puccini composed *Turandot* down to his hat and overcoat. Evidence of the national adulation he enjoyed is provided by the remarkable series of postcards which feature his haughty face – looking more like a business tycoon than a composer. There are also holograph letters and original costume designs used in his operas.

Corte San Lorenzo 9. Tel: (0583) 584 0287; www.casanatalepuccini.it. Open: Sept–May Tue–Sun 10am–1pm & 3–6pm; June–Aug daily 10am–6pm. Admission charge.

Duomo (Cathedral)

It is well worth pausing to look at the façade of the cathedral of San Martino before entering. Not only does this contain some of the most interesting details of the building; it also represents the last echo of the Romanesque style, which influenced churches all over Europe in the 10th to 13th centuries and which characterises so many of Lucca's fine churches.

The cathedral was founded in the 6th century and rebuilt between 1060 and 1070, although the façade was not added until 1204. The inlaid marble work on the façade is a *tour de force* and an excellent example of the so-called

The birthplace of the composer Puccini

Pisan Romanesque style. Among the best details are the bas-reliefs (by the left-hand door) showing the *Nativity* and the *Deposition*, attributed to Nicola Pisano. There is also a fascinating *Tree of Life*, with Adam and Eve at the bottom, and a series of panels depicting the labours of the months which provide a lively picture of everyday rural life in the 13th century.

The cathedral's interior was largely rebuilt between 1370 and 1490 and is rather gloomy. The dominant feature is the marble Tempietto or tabernacle (1484) by Matteo Civitali, Lucca's most important native artist. The Tempietto shelters one of Europe's most potent relics, the so-called *Volto Santo* or 'Holy Face'. The figure on the crucifix is said to be a true portrait of Christ, carved by Nicodemus, who witnessed the

Crucifixion and helped take Christ's body down from the Cross. Legend has it that the crucifix came to Lucca by supernatural means, and throughout the Middle Ages it was a major object of European pilgrimage – hence a considerable source of revenue to the cathedral authorities. Scholars now believe it was carved in the 12th or 13th century, but this does not deter the faithful who take part in a torchlight procession through the city, preceded by the holy image, every year on 13 September.

The low lighting makes it difficult to appreciate the remainder of the cathedral's interior details. On the third altar on the right is Tintoretto's *Last Supper*. The sacristy has a *Maesta* (Virgin Enthroned) by Ghirlandaio. The most beautiful object, however, is

The beautiful gardens at Palazzo Pfanner

the glimmering white marble tomb, in the left-hand aisle, of Ilaria del Carretto (1406), carved by the Sienese artist, Jacopo della Quercia. Ilaria, who died young, was the wife of Paolo Guinigi of the all-powerful clan that ruled Lucca. Della Quercia has shown her as an exquisitely graceful young woman asleep with her little dog at her feet.
Piazza San Martino. Tel: (0583) 490 530. Open: daily Dec–Feb 10am–5pm (2pm Mon–Fri); Mar–Nov 10am–6pm. Admission charge to sacristy.

Giardino Botanico (Botanical Garden)

Founded in 1820, this delightful garden is of great botanical interest and provides one of the few green areas within the city walls.
Via dell'Orto Botanico 14. Tel: (0583) 48785; www.operadellemura.it. Open: daily Apr 10am–5pm; May–June 10am–6pm; July–mid-Sept 10am–7pm; mid-Sept–Oct 10am–5pm. Open by appointment: Nov–Mar. Admission charge.

Museo dell'Opera del Duomo (Cathedral Works Museum)

This new museum shows how ultra-modern display techniques can be used to good effect in a medieval building. The museum houses the jewels which are used to decorate the *Volto Santo* on ceremonial occasions, and other objects are in the process of being transferred here from the cathedral.
Via Arcivescovado. Tel: (0583) 490 530;
www.museocattedralelucca.it. Open: daily Dec–Feb 10am–5pm (2pm Mon–Fri), Mar–Nov 10am–6pm. Admission charge.

Museo Nazionale (National Museum)

This museum is housed in the Villa Guinigi, another of the ruling family's town houses – this time an immense but plain Renaissance building in red brick tucked away on the eastern side of the town. The collection covers a wide range of displays, from archaeological finds to domestic furniture. There is a particularly interesting group of Romanesque reliefs. The picture gallery contains works by Lucchese and Sienese artists.
Via della Quarquonia. Tel: (0583) 496 033. Open: Tue–Sat 9am–7pm, Sun 9am–2pm. Admission charge.

Palazzo Pfanner

This museum has been restored and is well worth a visit. It houses a major collection of 17th- and 18th-century costume, including fine examples of the silk garments which made Lucca wealthy. The 18th-century garden (visible from the city walls) is small but delightfully laid out with statuary.
Via degli Asili 33. Open: daily mid-Mar–Oct 10am–6pm. Admission charge.

Piazza Napoleone

The dizzying political upheavals of the early 19th century turned Lucca into a

The façade of San Michele

Matteo Civitali (1435–1501). He began life as a barber, then became a sculptor and architect. Dominating the piazza is the church of San Michele in Foro with its truly amazing façade. This was built first and then the money ran out before the nave could be completed – that is why the upper section of the façade soars up into thin air. The figure of St Michael, flanked by trumpet-blowing angels, crowns the façade.

Pinacoteca Nazionale (National Art Gallery)

The main interest of this picture gallery is the building itself, the 17th-century Palazzo Mansi. Much of the original palace furnishings have survived and the focal point of interest is undoubtedly the bridal chamber and antechamber, a masterpiece of unrestrained vulgarity in gold and crimson velvet.

The paintings, with portraits predominating, are displayed much as they would have been when this was still in use as a family mansion. Among them are a number of Medici cardinals and Bronzino's portrait of Cosimo I, which fully brings out his ruthless nature.

Via Galli Tassi 43. Tel: (0583) 55570. Open: Tue–Sat 8.30am–7pm, Sun 8.30am–1pm. Admission charge.

San Frediano

This is another of Lucca's fine and unspoiled Romanesque churches, built between 1112 and 1147 and virtually

dukedom for the Bourbons in 1817. This sprawling, graceless square, largely used as a daytime car park, was their gift to the city. The immense building on the western side of the square was originally the seat of the republican council, but because it was occupied by the Bourbons it has been known as the Palazzo Ducale ever since. Despite its lack of architectural charm, the piazza is one of the liveliest places in Lucca. Immediately adjoining it is the Piazza del Giglio, site of Lucca's highly popular theatre, the Teatro Giglio.

Piazza San Michele

This piazza stands on the site of the Roman forum (*foro*) and it is still a popular meeting place for Lucca's citizens, testimony to the innate conservatism of Italian cities. In the loggia on the south side is a modern statue of Lucca's only major artist,

unaltered since. The façade is enlivened by a superb 13th-century mosaic of *The Ascension*, best seen after dark when the floodlighting creates a blaze of gold. The great font inside dates from the same period as the church, its carvings by at least three different artists, all anonymous but all of the first rank. In the chapel behind the font is displayed the 'uncorrupted' body of the patron saint of servants – St Zita, a pathetic mummy dressed up in incongruous finery, which is brought out on the saint's feast day (26 April) for the citizens to touch. In the neighbouring chapel are 16th-century frescoes depicting, among other subjects, the bringing of the *Volto Santo* to Lucca and San Frediano saving Lucca from a flood.
Piazza San Frediano. Tel: (0583) 493 627. Open: daily 9am–noon & 3.30–5pm. Free admission.

Santa Maria Forisportam

The main interest of this church lies in its name and its façade. Forisportam ('outside the gates') indicates that the church was built outside the first circuit of the Roman walls and gives some indication how the city has grown, for Santa Maria is now well within the main circuit. The façade is 13th-century Pisan Romanesque, unusually plain for that style, but harmonious.
Via Santa Croce.

Torre Guinigi (Guinigi's Tower)

It is not difficult to track down this massive town house of the Guinigi family because there is an oak tree growing from the top of its great tower. Built in red brick in the 14th century, the palace was the home of Lucca's ruling family. The great tower (*torre*) is open to the public and the remarkable little garden on the top, as well as the breathtaking views over the city, make it well worth a visit.
Casa Guinigi, via Sant'Andrea 41. Tel: (0583) 316 846. Open: daily June–15 Sept 9.30am–midnight; Nov–Feb 9.30am–5pm; Mar–May, 15 Sept–Oct 9.30am–8pm. Admission charge.

Torre Guinigi offers breathtaking views over Lucca

Walk: Lucca town walls

This walk takes you along the top of Lucca's well-preserved 16th-century city walls. Lucca's walls are so immense that they have a road along the top, some 4km (2½ miles) long, shaded by an avenue of trees. Walking the entire circuit is the best way to get a general view of the city. An added attraction, especially for children, is that you can hire bicycles to ride along the walls.

Allow 1 hour.

Lucca's walls, begun in 1500, took more than 150 years to build. Specifically designed to withstand an artillery attack, they are immensely thick, measuring 30m (98ft) wide at the base. Furthermore, the walls are surrounded by a complex system of earthworks and ditches: originally intended as part of the defences, they are now maintained as an attractive park separating the historic city centre from the chaotic ring road running around Lucca.

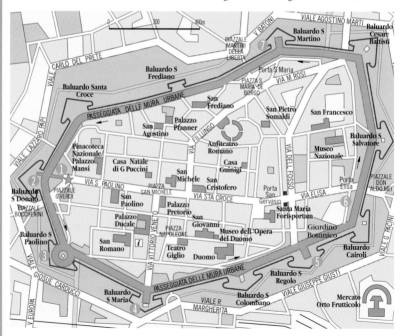

Regularly spaced along the walls are 11 immense spade-shaped *baluardi* (bastions) and six gates. Ironically, the walls were never attacked, so they are still in near-perfect condition.
Start at the Piazzale G Verdi.

1 Piazzale Giuséppe Verdi

You can hire bicycles near the tourist office in this piazza. The tourist office occupies one of the old city gates, which was superseded when the present circuit of walls was built.
Go up the ramp of the Baluardo San Donato, on the right of the city gate, then turn left to follow the Passeggiata delle Mura Urbane, the road that runs along the top of the walls.

2 Baluardo San Donato

The isolated building on the left is the headquarters of the Company of Lucchese Crossbowmen. Founded in 1443, the Company is still active, and in July puts on a splendid show at the Feast of San Paolino, the city's patron saint.

The wall plaque, put up in 1981, commemorates Castruccio Castracani who, in the early 14th century, freed Lucca from the control of Pisa and conquered a number of smaller surrounding cities.

3 Baluardo San Paolino

The next bastion is the headquarters of the International Institute for the Study of City Walls (CISCU). Within, the bastion is honeycombed with chambers and passages.

4 Baluardo Santa Maria

The next bastion is laid out as a lovely garden, with a café and a restaurant. As you continue walking, you will see the tall cathedral campanile on the left. From the next bastion, Baluardo San Colombano, you will get a good view of the cathedral itself.

5 Baluardo San Regolo

Here lies the entry to the Giardino Botanico (Botanical Garden, *see p95*). You can get a good view of the garden from a little further along the wall.

6 Porta Elisa

Just beyond the next bastion, Baluardo Cairoli, is one of the city gates, Porta Elisa. If you look left along the road which runs into the city from this gate you will see another massive gate, the Porta San Gervasio, part of the older city wall.
Continue on past Baluardo San Salvatore and Baluardo Cesare Battisti to Baluardo San Martino.

7 Baluardo San Martino

This protects one of the city's six gates, the Porta Santa Maria, which leads out on to a bustling piazza. A little further along, beyond the next bastion, the Baluardo San Frediano, there is an excellent view into the formal 18th-century garden of Palazzo Pfanner. Pass one more bastion, Santa Croce, and you will be back at the start.

Walk: Lucca town walls

Mercenaries

At the battle of Campaldino, fought in 1289 between Arezzo and Florence, the slaughter of citizen-soldiers on both sides was so great that it gave even the battle-hardened city-states pause for thought. From that time on, mercenaries gradually began to take over the fighting. These mercenaries were often foreign (a foreign soldier was regarded as having no interest in local politics), with English, Germans and Hungarians predominating. They formed themselves into companies of about 5,000 men under the command of a *condottiere*, so-called because he would negotiate a *condotta* (a form of contract) with a particular city; this stipulated that his company would serve the city for a set period of time for a set sum. When that period was finished, the *condottiere* was free to find another employer – even if (as was often the case) this was the enemy of their previous employer.

The main aim of every mercenary was to avoid being killed while making a lot of money. Wars between city-states came to resemble a chess game with formalised moves. Bribery was common and the cities were obliged to raise the stakes ever higher simply to retain the status quo.

One *condottiere* who could not be bribed once he had signed a *condotta* was the feared Englishman, John Hawkwood, whom the Tuscans nicknamed Giovanni Acuto (literally John Sharp). Born in Essex in about 1320, he fought in France under the Black Prince. During one of the truces of the Hundred Years War he travelled to Italy and formed the White Company, composed of discharged English soldiers.

Hawkwood was a rarity among *condottieri* in that, as well as not being tempted by bribes, he always honoured his contract. In 1377 the Florentines made him their Captain General, in supreme command of all military forces in the city and even, on occasions, charged with policing the turbulent citizens. The city council promised him a handsome equestrian statue after his death. When the time came, however, they thriftily decided to settle for a wall painting instead. They did, though, commission Paolo Uccello to paint this commemorative fresco, which can be seen in Florence Cathedral (*see p48*). Uccello used the new chiaroscuro technique, which at least gave the fresco the appearance of a three-dimensional stone monument.

Sir John Hawkwood

Montepulciano

Apart from the peace, and its famous Vino Nobile, Montepulciano's chief attraction is architectural, for it is a perfect miniature Renaissance city with a remarkable number of outstanding palaces. Many are the work of the Florentine architect, Antonio Sangallo the Elder (1455–1537), who came to Montepulciano in 1511.

Traffic has been almost totally banned from Montepulciano and the best way to explore the city is to follow the Corso, the wide main road which winds up from Porta al Prato gate at the lower end of the town round to the Piazza Grande on the crest of the hill.

119km (74 miles) southeast of Florence, 36km (22 miles) southeast of Siena. Montepulciano is about one and a half hours by bus from Siena. The nearest railway station is Chiusi-Chianciano (11km/7 miles away), on the Siena to Rome line. Buses connect this station to Montepulciano. Tourist Information Office: Piazza Don Minzoni 1. Tel: (0578) 757 341; www.comune.montepulciano.si.it

Montepulciano

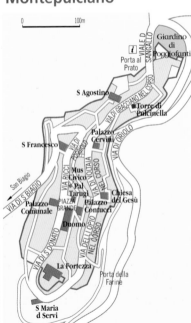

Duomo (Cathedral)

The elegant late Renaissance cathedral has one outstanding work of art: the *Assumption of the Virgin* altarpiece by Taddeo di Bartolo (1401).
Piazza Grande. Open: daily.
Free admission.

Museo Civico (Town Museum)

The most interesting feature of this museum is probably the building itself. This is one of Montepulciano's many

fine palaces, the Palazzo Neri-Orselli, built in the Sienese Gothic style. The collection includes some terracottas from the della Robbia workshops, and a number of paintings, mostly 16th century, by local artists.
Via Ricci 10. Tel: (0578) 717 300. Open: Oct–Mar Tue–Sun 10am–1pm & 3–6pm; Apr–Sept until 7pm; Aug daily 10am–7pm. Admission charge.

Palazzo Comunale

Montepulciano's little 14th-century Palazzo Comunale is a flattering copy of the Palazzo Vecchio in Florence. It achieved this appearance when the façade was remodelled in the 15th century by the Florentine architect, Michelozzo. The tower is the main attraction and the ascent, via a number of ladders, is an interesting experience in its own right; from the top there is a superb view of the town.
Piazza Grande 1. Tel: (0578) 712 034. Open: Mon–Sat 8am–1pm. Free admission.

Piazza Grande

Laid out like a stage set on the highest point of the hill on which Montepulciano sits, this is the city's main square. Look out for the splendid lion and griffin fountain in the northeast corner of the square, in front of the arcaded Palazzo Tarugi.

Porta al Prato

Montepulciano was a prize over which both Florence and Siena fought. As soon as Florence gained control, Antonio Sangallo was sent to strengthen its defences. This great gate, which is still the main entrance to the town, was his first work. Just beyond the gate is the Florentine symbol, the *marzocco*, a heraldic lion (the original is in the Museo Civico).

San Biagio

You will have to leave the town to visit this church for it stands just outside the city walls to the southwest and is approached along an avenue of cypresses. It is well worth the half-hour walk, for not only is this Antonio Sangallo's masterpiece but it is also set in beautiful rural surroundings.
Via di San Biagio 14. Open: daily 8am–7pm. Free admission.

Torre di Pulcinella

This is one of Montepulciano's few surviving tower houses, dating back to the turbulent medieval period. On the roof is Pulcinella the clown, one of the characters from the Commedia dell'Arte, which strikes the hours on the town bell.
Piazza Michelozzo.

Architectural beauty in every corner

Pisa

There is far more to Pisa than the famous Leaning Tower, yet the city suffers from a low profile. Visitors tend to arrive at the airport and spend perhaps a couple of hours in and around the Campo dei Miracoli before rushing off by train or coach to Florence or Siena.

Pisa town plan

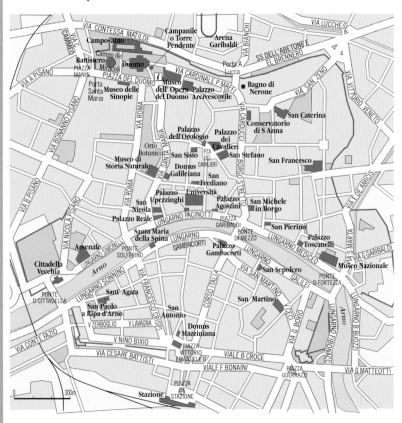

In part this is because Pisa is overshadowed by Florence, barely an hour away by train. But nature has also conspired against it. Whereas in Florence the Arno is still a living river crossed by four elegant and historic bridges, the Arno in Pisa is a sullen brown flood which is bordered by low-rise buildings and crossed by a series of nondescript modern bridges.

History

No one knows the precise origins of Pisa. Bronze Age artefacts have been discovered near the city and there are claims that Pisa was founded by the ancient Greeks. Roman remains, among them the ruins of the so-called Bagno di Nerone (Baths of Nero) in Largo del Parlascio, show that this was an important imperial city.

But Pisa's great period began in the 11th century when, in a series of tremendous sea battles against Arabic ships, she won control of the western Mediterranean.

In 1069, by defeating the Saracens of Sicily, the city won so colossal a booty it paid for the superb buildings on the Campo dei Miracoli, which launched an entirely new form of architecture.

For the next 300 years or so, Pisa remained one of the great maritime cities of the Mediterranean, but unfortunately drawn into endless battles with neighbouring cities, it eventually fell to Florence in 1406.

Pisa ceased to be a major port in the 16th century when Livorno became the main harbour in Tuscany. Since then the city has declined and, in the 19th century, the poet Percy Bysshe Shelley described it as 'a desolation of a city, which was the cradle and is now the grave of a distinguished people'.

In the closing months of World War II, the city was at the front line of the fighting between the advancing Allies and the retreating Germans, who faced each other on either side of the Arno; Allied bombers attacked the city in 1943, and it suffered terribly as a consequence.

Today, Pisa has been rebuilt and is an important industrial and university city, one of the largest in Tuscany, with a population of over 100,000.

Orientation

The historic city centre is concentrated on the north bank of the river and is still surrounded by 12th-century walls. The 'high street' is the long and curving Via Santa Maria, which connects the Campo dei Miracoli with the Lungarno (Embankment).

The palaces and mansions that line this street still retain their handsome façades dating from the 16th to the 18th centuries. No 25 (built in 1595) has the bust of Duke Ferdinand I, while the building at the end of the street is the Palazzo Reale, the royal palace of the Grand Dukes.

No 26 is the Domus Galileiana, named after Galileo, an 18th-century building which once housed the Observatory and is now a scientific research centre.

The social centre of Pisa is the Piazza Garibaldi on the north side of the Ponte di Mezzo (Middle Bridge) and the elegant colonnaded Borgo Stretto which leads away from it.

Pisa is 91km (56½ miles) west of Florence. Pisa Centrale station is on the main railway line between Galileo Galilei airport (Pisa Aeroporto station) and Florence. Tourist Information Office: Via Silvio Pellico 6. Tel: (050) 929 777; www.pisaturismo.it

Battistero (Baptistery)

Begun in 1152 by Diotisalvi, the main body of the Baptistery was not completed until 1284 after Nicola Pisano and his son, Giovanni, added the splendid Gothic arcades of the upper storey. Even then, the Baptistery

The Baptistery, like a papal crown

COMBINED TICKET

You can save a considerable sum of money by buying a combined ticket to the major attractions of the Campo dei Miracoli. The ticket can be bought at any of the participating sights and covers admission to the Museo delle Sinopie, the Museo dell'Opera del Duomo, the Battistero and the Camposanto (the Duomo is free). *www.opapisa.it*

---

did not take its final form until the Gothic dome was added in the 14th century. The Pisani also carved the figures in the entrance portals (most of these are copies; the originals are now in the Museo dell'Opera del Duomo (*see p109*). The circular shape of the Baptistery was inspired by the Church of the Holy Sepulchre in Jerusalem and, because only a segment is visible at a time from outside, on stepping inside you receive the extraordinary impression that the immense interior is bigger than the exterior. The Baptistery, Italy's largest, is famous for its acoustics and is virtually empty of furnishings except for the font by Guido da Como (1246) and Nicola Pisano's superb pulpit (1260). It is worth ascending the ramp within the Baptistery walls to reach the upper gallery to get a bird's-eye view of the building, and the unusual view of the Duomo façade. *Campo dei Miracoli. Tel: (050) 387 2211; www.opapisa.it. Open: daily Mar & Oct 9am–6pm, Nov–Feb 10am–5pm, Apr–Sept 8am–8pm. Last entry: 40 minutes before closing time. Admission charge.*

Campanile (The Leaning Tower)

Work began on Pisa's famous Leaning Tower in 1173. By the time the tower had reached about a third of its intended height it began to lean because of the sandy and unstable nature of the subsoil. In attempting to correct this fault, successive architects built back at an angle so that the profile of the tower is, in fact, a shallow crescent. The tower was completed around 1350, since when it has continued to tilt; the angle at which it is leaning is now 5.2m (17ft) from the perpendicular, and steadily increasing. Experts predict that the tower will eventually collapse, and for at least the last 100 years architects of all nations have put forward various suggestions for checking the incline. The most recent effort involving a combination of lead weights and soil extraction has successfully reversed the tilt, hopefully adding centuries to the tower's life and making it stable enough for visits from the public.

Campo dei Miracoli. Tel: (050) 387 2211. Open: daily with guides Nov–Feb 10am–5pm; Mar 9am–6pm; Apr–Sept 8.30am–8.30pm; mid-June–Aug 8.30am–11pm; Oct 9am–7pm. Children under 8 years of age not allowed. Advance booking at www.opapisa.it; www.leaningtowerpisa.it

Campo dei Miracoli (The Field of Miracles)

This is Pisa's great set piece, an immense green lawn on which stand four great buildings in gleaming white marble – the Duomo (Cathedral), the Battistero (Baptistery), the Campanile (Leaning Tower) and the Camposanto (Cemetery). Surrounding the Campo on two sides is the city wall. There are also two major museums on the south side: the **Museo delle Sinopie** contains the original sketches in plaster from the fire-damaged frescoes of the Camposanto (*open: summer 9am–7pm, winter 9am–6pm*), and the Museo dell'Opera del Duomo (*see p109*).

Camposanto (Holy Field)

Camposanto literally means 'Holy Field' and this site was chosen as the city's main cemetery in the 13th century. It consists essentially of a rectangular cloister, built between the late 13th and early 15th centuries, surrounding a

Famously leaning, Pisa's Romanesque campanile was begun in 1173

simple garden. According to legend, earth for the cemetery was brought back from the Holy Land in the 13th century to be used for important burials.

Pisan notables, mostly clerical, are still buried here, and the cloister has an outstanding range of funerary monuments, from ancient Roman sarcophagi to modern sculptures.

An Allied bomb destroyed most of the frescoes which once covered the walls. Those that survived include a substantial part of *The Triumph of Death*, painted by an unknown master and commemorating the Black Death of 1348. For protection, this has been removed and placed under cover in one of the chambers off the north side of the cloister.

There is also a display here of black-and-white photographs showing the frescoes before the destruction.

Pisa's Duomo

GALILEO GALILEI (1564–1642)

Galileo, the great mathematician and astronomer, and father of empirical science, was born in Pisa. Legend has it that he got the idea of the pendulum while observing the great lamp swinging in the cathedral. He also tested his theory of the speed of falling objects by dropping them from the Leaning Tower.

The Inquisition condemned him for heresy in teaching that the earth went round the sun and not vice versa, and he was denied a Christian burial until 1737. In 1992, the Vatican finally conceded that his theory was correct.

Campo dei Miracoli. Tel: (050) 387 2211; www.opapisa.it. Open: same as Baptistery. Last entry: 40 minutes before closing time.

Duomo (Cathedral)

Begun in 1063, Pisa's cathedral brings together three distinct architectural traditions – Roman, Islamic and Byzantine – fused together to create a unique new style, Pisan Romanesque. The 12th-century bronze doors of the Portale di San Ranieri (opposite the Leaning Tower) are the work of Bonanno da Pisa (the original architect of the tower); these too demonstrate Pisan acquaintance with the Eastern Mediterranean, in the palm trees and other realistic details in the background to the biblical scenes. A disastrous fire in 1595 destroyed most of the works of art in the cathedral. Among the survivors is the monumental pulpit by Giovanni Pisano (1302–10). It was removed after the fire and forgotten – it was not rediscovered and replaced until

1926. Other survivals include the great mosaic of *Christ Enthroned* by Cimabue (1302) in the apse, and the noble tomb of the Holy Roman Emperor, Henry VII, who died in Pisa in 1313.
Campo dei Miracoli. Tel: (050) 387 2211; www.opapisa.it. Open: Mar & Oct Mon–Sat 10am–6pm; Nov–Feb Mon–Sat 10am–1pm, 2–5pm; Apr–Sept Mon–Sat 10am–8pm. Free admission.

Lungarni (Embankments)

The embankments running alongside the Arno are lined with 16th-century palaces. Near the Ponte della Cittadella on the north bank is the Arsenal of the Medici. Behind the 18th-century façade at Lungarno Pacinotti 44 is a medieval tower house, while the façade of No 26 is a remarkable terracotta confection of the late 13th century. Just to the north of this embankment is the Palazzo Sapienza, the principal offices of Pisa's university, originally built in the 14th century, and expanded by the Medici. At Lungarno Mediceo 30 (beyond Piazza Garibaldi) is the largely 16th-century Palazzo Toscanelli which Byron rented in 1821.

On the south bank, near the Ponte Solferino, the 14th-century church of Santa Maria della Spina stands in isolated splendour.

Museo dell'Opera del Duomo (Cathedral Works Museum)

This excellent modern museum occupies the original chapterhouse of the cathedral. There are intimate views of the Leaning Tower from the cloister. The museum contains numerous works of art, including fine sculptures by the Pisani dating from the foundation of the cathedral down to the 19th century. On the upper floor is a brilliant display of coloured 19th-century engravings of the frescoes in the Camposanto, showing just what has been lost.
Piazza Arcivescovado, near the Leaning Tower. Tel: (050) 560 547. Open: same as Baptistery. Tel: (050) 387 2211; www.opapisa.it. Admission charge.

Orto Botanico (Botanical Garden)

This delightful green spot is one of the oldest botanical gardens in Europe, founded in the 1540s.
Via L Ghini 5, just off Via S Maria. Tel: (050) 221 5374. Open: Mon–Sat 8am–1pm. Closed: Sun. Free admission.

Piazza dei Cavalieri

The original central square of medieval Pisa, the Piazza dei Cavalieri, was also probably the site of the Roman forum. Vasari redesigned the square for Duke Cosimo I, whose statue stands in front of the strangely decorated Palazzo dei Cavalieri. To the left of this building is the Palazzo dell'Orologio, built in 1607 and incorporating the remains of a medieval tower. Dante tells the grim story of how Count Ugolino della Gherardesca, along with his sons and grandsons, was starved to death in 1288 by being walled up in this tower, having been tried on false treason charges.

San Gimignano

As you approach San Gimignano, the distant view of this little town, with its soaring slender towers, looks just like an illumination found in a medieval manuscript. San Gimignano is commonly referred to as the 'city of the beautiful towers', but these stern structures were not built for aesthetic reasons.

All Tuscan towns once had such towers, which are evidence of the violent conditions of life in medieval Italy. Each belonged to a family or a corporation, desperately striving to rise above their neighbours so that they could better defend themselves during

San Gimignano

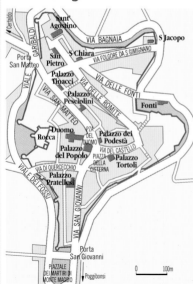

times of riot by dropping missiles or burning pitch or oil on the enemy. Incredibly, there were once over 70 towers in this tiny hilltop town (compared with 100 in Florence), of which 13 survive.

San Gimignano has reversed the normal Tuscan trend, for its present population of around 7,500 is half what it was in the 16th century. It is small enough to be explored in a day.
55km (34 miles) southwest of Florence, 38km (24 miles) northwest of Siena. Scores of tour operators in Florence and Siena run daily excursions to San Gimignano, but there are no regular bus services from either city.
Tourist Information Office: Piazza del Duomo 1. Tel: (0577) 940 008; www.sangimignano.com

Collegiata (Collegiate Church)
San Gimignano's collegiate church is often called the Duomo (Cathedral) even though the town no longer has a bishop. The plain brick exterior of

the 12th-century church gives no hint of the richness of its interior.

The entire expanse of the great nave walls is covered with a series of murals. The best time to see them is early in the morning, for there is little by way of natural light.

The northern wall, painted in the 1360s by Bartolo di Fredi, illustrates events from the Old Testament.

The southern wall illustrates the life of Christ. Also in this aisle is the Santa Fina Chapel, with charming frescoes on the life of this female saint by the Florentine artist, Ghirlandaio.

On the west wall, high above the entrance, is a particularly horrific *Last Judgement* (1393) by Taddeo di Bartolo, showing the damned being punished. *Piazza del Duomo. Tel: (0577) 940 316. Open: Mar–Oct Mon–Fri 9.30am–7.30pm, Sat 9.30am–5pm, Sun 1–5pm; Nov–Feb Mon–Sat 9.30am–5pm, Sun 1–5pm. Free admission (except for the Santa Fina Chapel).*

Museo Civico (Civic Museum)

This museum is situated in the Palazzo del Popolo, itself a fine medieval building. Its main room is the Sala di Dante, so called because Dante, as the ambassador of Florence, delivered a speech here in 1300 arguing the case for Guelf unity. The walls have 13th- and 14th-century frescoes.

On the left of the main staircase a plain little room contains two famous frescoes by Memmo di Filippuccio

depicting domestic life. Known as the 'Wedding Frescoes', they show the bride and groom taking a bath together, and in bed.

In the adjoining picture gallery a painting of San Gimignano, the town's patron saint, shows him holding a model of the town in his hands; the painting dates from the late 14th century and shows how little San Gimignano's appearance has altered since. The staircase continues up the Torre Grossa, the highest of the town's surviving towers and the only one open to the public. *Piazza del Duomo. Tel: (0577) 940 340. Open: daily Mar–Oct 9.30am–7.20pm, Nov–Feb 10am–5.50pm. Admission charge.*

Rocca

Little remains of this 14th-century castle, but the interior has been turned into a pleasant public park. *Behind the Collegiata. Open: 24 hours.*

Sant'Agostino

This huge 13th-century church hides a treasure of Renaissance painting just behind the high altar. This is Benozzo Gozzoli's *Life of Saint Augustine*. *Piazza Sant'Agostino. Open: daily 7.30am–noon & 3–7pm. Free admission.*

Walk: San Gimignano country

This walk through the countryside around San Gimignano is especially pleasant in the autumn when the vineyards around the town are full of ripe grapes.

Allow 5 hours for the main walk or 1½ hours for the shorter alternative.

Main walk

Leave San Gimignano by the Porta San Matteo. Follow Via Garibaldi to the right, beneath the high walls around San Gimignano. After 100m (110yds), take the first left, then shortly after turn right, taking the road leading north towards Casale and Sant'Andrea. Beware of heavy traffic along the first stretch of this route, but do stop to look back at the incredible skyline of San Gimignano with the towers apparently

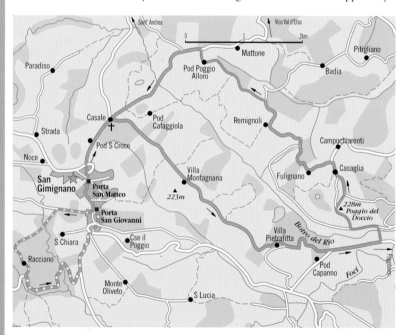

springing straight up from the vineyards. After 1km (½ mile) you will come to a junction with a little rural church on the right. Take the right-hand turning to walk along an unmetalled road signposted to Villa Pietrafitta. There is virtually no traffic along this track so you can walk at leisure, admiring the tremendous views over the valley to the right of the vineyards that surround San Gimignano, famous for their Vernaccia wine, a crisp dry white.

San Gimignano nestles within vine-rich countryside

Villa Pietrafitta is reached after 3.5km (2 miles). Continue 750m (820yds) through the hamlet until you join the main road linking San Gimignano to Poggibonsi. Follow this road leftward (towards Poggibonsi) for just under 1km (½ mile), then take the first left downhill and over a bridge across the Botro del Rio (the Rio Ravine). Once over the bridge turn left and then, after 500m (547yds), turn right to climb the hill called Poggio del Doccio (228m/784ft). Near the crest of the hill the road forks: take the right branch through Casaglia. At the far side of this hamlet, the road branches again: turn left and follow the twisting rural road running along the northeastern side of the Vergaia valley. After 3km (2 miles) you meet the main San Gimignano to Vico Val d'Elsa road. Turn left and follow this all the way uphill to San Gimignano.

Shorter route

For a quicker introduction to the countryside, leave San Gimignano by

the Porta San Giovanni. Turn right immediately outside the gate and cross to the car park to the right of Viale dei Fossi. Take the steep downhill track running by the side of the car park.

This takes you, within minutes, into beautiful open country with a dramatic backward view of the town. Continue down the road for 1km (½ mile) until it terminates in a farmyard. Take the left fork here to follow a rough farm track for about 2km (1 mile). The track now joins a metalled lane: bear left and continue up the hill, where you will reach the large vineyard of Racciano after 250m (273yds).

The road now runs another 250m (273yds) along the crest of the hill, offering wide views on each side, then plunges down through the vineyards. In autumn, just before the *vendemmia* (harvest), when the vines are heavy with fruit, this is a particularly attractive walk.

The lane now joins the main road to Volterra. Turn left and follow the road uphill. After 2km (1 mile) you will regain the Porta San Giovanni.

Siena

At almost every point, Siena is the opposite of its Tuscan rival, Florence. Where Florentine buildings are classically inspired and built of brown or grey stone, Siena's are Gothic and built of reddish-brown brick, the colour known to artists as 'burnt siena'. Where Florence is dour and masculine, its streets bustling with nervous activity, Siena is graceful and feminine.

Looking round this exquisite little hilltop city, with its population of 60,000 (as opposed to Florence's 380,000), it is hard to imagine that, in the Middle Ages, Siena fought it out on equal terms with Florence, with the

Siena town plan

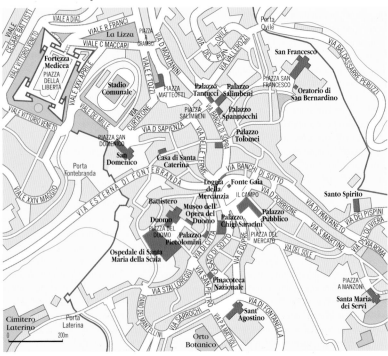

balance more than once tipping in her favour. Gradually, however, the sheer power and wealth of Florence and the sheer cunning and skill of its politicians wore down its rival.

The final battle took place in 1555 and it has been estimated that Siena lost 60 per cent of its population in this last long and bloody contest. Having conquered Siena, the Medici Dukes covered it with their boastful insignia and then pursued a deliberate policy of suppressing Sienese business and initiative. Siena did not die, for it has a tremendous inner vitality, but it did become a backwater for nearly four centuries.

Siena is built on six hills – this means that parts of it have the curious trick of appearing and disappearing like a city in some fairytale.

Some viewpoints will unexpectedly present Siena's dramatic skyline in its entirety while from others you can catch refreshing glimpses of open country. Siena's streets are much narrower than those of Florence and they are arched over in many places, which creates a tunnel-like effect; even so, there is no feeling of claustrophobia and the vista is constantly changing.
Siena is 68km (42 miles) south of Florence. Trains run roughly every hour to Siena from Florence, changing at Empoli (journey time 90 minutes). There is also a fast and regular bus service between Florence and Siena. Tourist Information Office: Piazza del Campo 56. Tel: (0577) 280 551; www.terresiena.it

Battistero (Baptistery)

Unusually for Tuscany, Siena's Baptistery is not a separate building. It is located at the east end of the cathedral, where the crypt would normally be, with a separate entrance at ground level, emphasising the steepness of the hill on which the whole structure is built. The Baptistery's supreme work of art is the great font.

Florence and Siena might have been deadly political rivals, but in the freemasonry of art they did not hesitate to employ each other's great artists, and both Ghiberti and Donatello contributed to the sculptures on the font.
Piazza San Giovanni. Tel: (0577) 283 048; www.operaduomo.siena.it. Open: daily June–Aug 9.30am–8pm; Mar–May & Sept–Oct 9am–7.30pm; Nov–Feb 10am–5pm. Admission charge. Joint ticket available for Cathedral, Baptistery and Museo dell'Opera.

Il Campo (The Field)

Completed by the year 1349 – just a year after the Black Death struck Tuscany – this vast shell-shaped piazza is the very heart of Siena and one of the most perfect public squares in all Italy. The Campo is paved in the same harmonious reddish-brown brick as the city's medieval buildings, and it slopes downwards, forming a kind of amphitheatre, with the Palazzo Pubblico as the stage. It is surrounded by buildings on all sides; access to the Campo is through narrow arched alleys so that visually the square looks completely enclosed.

The only monument in the piazza itself is the Fonte Gaia. This is a copy (made in 1868) of the original fountain that was carved between 1408 and 1419 by Siena's greatest sculptor, Jacopo della Quercia. The remains of the badly eroded original panels are now displayed on the loggia of the Palazzo Pubblico.

The Campo is also the location of Tuscany's most famous festival – Il Palio (see pp148–9).

Duomo (Cathedral)

The interior of most Italian cathedrals tends to be somewhat bare, but Siena's is an exception. In fact, it is so crammed with interest that the best thing to do is to drop in for half an hour or so at a time – the generous opening hours make this possible. The interior is very dark so you will need a good supply of coins for the automatic lights.

The cathedral is a vast building, but not big enough for the tastes of the Sienese, who had no sooner completed this great building than they decided they wanted a bigger one. Work was started on a new structure in 1339 but was brought to a halt by the Black Death of 1348. The enormous walls on the right-hand side (south) of the cathedral square are all that was completed of this ambitious project.

The striking black and white stripes of the cathedral's exterior are continued into the interior, to dazzling effect. Ranged high up around the nave is the most bizarre feature of even this

POPE PIUS II

Aeneas Silvius Piccolomini was born in 1405 and came from a rich Sienese banking family. He travelled widely throughout Europe as a papal emissary, and then became both secretary and court poet to the Holy Roman Emperor, Frederick III of Germany. He entered the priesthood quite late in life, was made bishop of Trieste, and then, in 1456, appointed a cardinal. Two years later, in 1458, he was elected Pope Pius II. During his six-year reign he made a great effort to introduce reforms into the Church. In Tuscany he created the beautiful little Renaissance town of Pienza, an early example of a planned town. His letters are delightfully readable and provide an insight into the Renaissance papacy.

remarkable building – polychrome busts of every pope who had ever reigned, from St Peter up to the mid-16th century.

Of far greater artistic merit is Nicola Pisano's superb pulpit. Completed in 1268, it is similar to his great pulpit in Pisa's Baptistery, with pillars supported by lions and dramatic relief sculptures.

The marble pavement of the nave is a unique and extraordinarily detailed work. Created between 1369 and 1547, it is said that every artist active in the city worked on these pictures at some stage.

Altogether there are 56 scenes, ranging from simple black and white outlines to complex multicoloured pictures in marble. In order to protect them, the cathedral authorities have covered some with hardboard, but some of the more interesting scenes are simply roped off. These include the elaborate Massacre of the Innocents scene near Pisano's pulpit and the fascinating black and white *Allegory of Fortune* by Pinturicchio, located in the centre of the nave; nobody knows the precise meaning of some of the scenes portrayed in this allegory, but that does not make it any the less enjoyable. The whole of the pavement is uncovered between mid-August and mid-October (the exact dates change year by year), and there is an admission charge during that period.

Pinturicchio's work appears again in full glory in the Libreria Piccolomini, whose entrance is on the left-hand (north) side of the nave. Here you can enjoy one of the most complete and beautiful displays of Renaissance painting to come from the hands of one man. The library was built in 1495 to house the books collected by the learned pope and humanist, Pius II. In ten great panels painted in vibrant and luminous colour, Pinturicchio has illustrated scenes from the life of the pope, including his visit to James II of Scotland, his canonisation of Siena's own saint, Catherine, and the last, sad event of his life when he waited in vain at Ancona for the ships of the Christian powers who had promised to join his Crusade against the Turks.

In 2004, the 13th-century crypt opened to the public in all its painted glory. The gold, blues and reds of the beautiful frescoes survived almost intact for centuries, having been hidden from view and tightly sealed until their discovery in 2000.

Piazza del Duomo. Tel: (0577) 283 048; www.operaduomo.siena.it. Cathedral: open Mon–Sat 10.30am–7.30pm (Nov–Feb 6.30pm), Sun 1.30–5.30pm (June–Aug 6pm). Library: open mid-Mar–Oct Mon–Sat 9am–7.30pm, Sun 2–7.30pm; Nov–mid-Mar Mon–Sat 10am–1pm & 2–5pm, Sun 2–5pm. Admission charge.

Forte di Santa Barbara/Fortezza Medicea (Saint Barbara Fort)

The great fortress that dominates the western approach to Siena was built in 1560 by Duke Cosimo I, and is one of several castles he had constructed to

Façade of the Cathedral in Siena

hold down the cities he conquered. Today, the garden within the castle walls forms a pleasant and shady retreat. The bastion facing into the gardens of La Lizza houses a wine bar and shop called **Enoteca Italiana** (*see p161*), with an immense stock of wines from all over Italy (*open: Apr–Sept Mon noon–8pm, Tue–Sat noon–1am; Oct–Mar Tue–Wed noon–8pm, Thur–Sat noon–1am*). The landscaped path running along the top of the castle walls provides excellent views of the city.
Piazza della Libertà. Tel: (0577) 288 811; www.enoteca-italiana.it.
Free admission.

Loggia della Mercanzia (Merchants' Lodge)

Situated where the three main streets of central Siena meet, this was a natural spot for merchants to gather. The loggia was built in the early 15th century and has recently been restored.
Via di Città 3/5.

Museo dell'Opera del Duomo (Cathedral Works Museum)

This museum is housed in the bricked-up aisle to the right (south) of the Duomo, thus occupying part of the new cathedral that was planned but never finished. The ground floor is occupied by displays of 13th- and 14th-century statuary taken down from the façade of the cathedral. They include works by Giovanni Pisano and Siena's own Jacopo della Quercia. On the first floor is the Sala di Duccio in which the

work of Siena's greatest artist, Duccio di Buoninsegna, is displayed in an almost religious atmosphere of low lighting and hushed voices. Pride of place, in a blaze of gold, is given to the great *Maestà* – the Enthroned Virgin – completed in 1311. Opposite are scenes from the Life of Christ, also by Duccio. These lively vignettes dispel the idea that early Sienese art lacks humour and realism. In *Peter Denying Christ* a group of men huddle round a fire while a servant girl points accusingly at Peter, who holds up his hand in denial.

In the rooms above are further works of art, including the so-called *Madonna degli Occhi Grossi* (Madonna of the Large Eyes), painted between 1220 and 1230 in the formal Byzantine style from which Gothic art developed. In the same room is an extraordinary reliquary with the skull and bones of some anonymous saint tied up with ribbons like a Christmas parcel. From the Sala dei Parati, where vestments are displayed, a small door leads to a staircase and viewpoint high up on the unfinished façade of the planned new cathedral. From here there are superb views.
Piazza del Duomo 8. Tel: (0577) 283 048; www.operaduomo.siena.it. See hours for Baptistery (p115). Admission charge.

Palazzo Chigi–Saracini (Chigi–Saracini Palace)

Like the Piccolomini, the Chigi were one of the great banking families of Siena with a foothold in the papacy. Their handsome 14th-century palace is now the seat of the highly regarded musical academy, the Accademia Musicale Chigiana. The vast musical library is open to the public and you can walk into the beautiful inner courtyard. On display there is usually a list of the concerts sponsored by the Academy.

Via di Città 89. Tel: (0577) 22091; www.chigiani.it. Open: Mon–Fri Sept–June 9.30am–12.30pm; Mon–Fri July–Aug 10am–1pm & 3.30–5pm.

Palazzo Piccolomini (Piccolomini Palace)

This is the most important of the three palaces which the Piccolomini pope, Pius II, built for his family in the city (the palace he built for his sister, irreverently known as the Palazzo delle Papesse – the Palace of the She-popes – is opposite the Palazzo Chigi-Saracini).

This palazzo is the work of the Florentine architect, Bernardo Rossellino, who also designed the city of Pienza. Today, the palace houses the state archives (Archivo di Stato di Siena). The great interest here is the series of painted wooden covers used to bind the city's medieval account books, the *Biccherna* and the *Gabelle*, which are works of art in their own right. They are exhibited in the Sala di Congresso, which is open to the public.

Via Banchi di Sotto 52. Tel: (0577) 247 145; http://assi.archivi.beniculturali.it. Open: Mon–Sat with 3 timed visits at 9.30am, 10.30am, 11.30am. Free admission.

Palazzo Pubblico (Public Palace)

Siena's grand city hall forms the perfect centrepiece of the city's majestic piazza, known simply as Il Campo (The Field, *see pp115–16*). Completed in the 1340s, the building was so admired that it influenced the design of all the other

The Torre del Mangia, Siena's most distinctive landmark, rises high above the city

buildings around the piazza, as well as buildings all over Siena.

The incredible campanile, known as the Torre del Mangia, is the second tallest in Italy and rises to 102m (335ft). The climb to the top is well worth the effort because of the stupendous views that open out. At the base of the tower is the Cappella di Piazza, a small chapel built during 1352–76 in the form of an open loggia in thanksgiving for the end of the Black Death. As with most of Italy's historic city halls, the Palazzo Pubblico is still the centre of local government, but its main historic rooms now serve as the city's Museo Civico. The displays consist largely of *in situ* frescoes and they should not on any account be missed because they sum up, in dramatic and understandable form, vital periods in Italian history.

The museum is approached up a modern steel staircase, past a well-run museum shop, but then immediately takes you back into the past. The ceiling and walls of the first room are painted with scenes illustrating key moments in the *Risorgimento* – the long and often bitter struggle that finally led to Italy achieving unification in 1870. The major figures depicted here are Garibaldi and Vittorio Emanuele II, the first king of modern Italy.

The next important room is the Sala del Mappamondo which houses the great, recently restored *Maestà* by Simone Martini. On the opposite wall is another great fresco, showing the *condottiere* (mercenary), Guidoriccio da Fogliano, setting off for battle in his full military regalia. Beyond, in the Sala dei Nove (Room of the Nine), are the *Allegories of Good and Bad Government*

The Palazzo Pubblico, Siena

by Ambrogio Lorenzetti. Commissioned in 1338, these were intended to remind Siena's governing Council of Nine, who used the room for their meetings, of the consequences of their decisions. *Good Government* is shown as a resolute, bearded figure flanked and supported by all the Virtues while the citizens of Siena happily go about their daily affairs. The fresco presents a marvellous picture of ordinary life in the 14th century. *Bad Government* is characterised by the figure of fear presiding over a ruined countryside where murder, robbery and rape run riot.

Piazza del Campo 1.
Tel: (0577) 292 263;
www.comune.siena.it/museocivico.
Museum: open daily mid-Mar–Oct
10am–7pm; Nov–mid-Mar
10am–6.30pm. Tower: open daily mid-
Mar–Oct 10am–7pm; Nov–mid-Mar
10am–4pm. Last entry: 45 minutes
before closing time. Admission charge.

Interior of the Duomo, Siena

Pinacoteca Nazionale (National Art Gallery)

The pictures in this art gallery demonstrate how Sienese art developed along different lines from that of Florence. Artists of the Sienese school were renowned for their delicate and mystical paintings, many depicting the Virgin, patron saint of the city, as can be seen by the many altarpieces exhibited.

In Room 2 there are some lively little panel pictures from the 13th century, whose very crudity of detail is attractive. Among them, for instance, is *The Story of Four Saints* showing a strange obsession with torture. Highlights of the collection include the *Adoration of the Magi* by Bartolo di Fredi (1330–1410), showing a contemporary view of Siena, and the portrait of the Borgia pope Calixtus III by Sano di Pietro (1406–81), which also has Siena as the background.

The top floor of the gallery houses the Collezione Spannocchi, an important collection of small paintings by non-Italian artists, including Dürer's *St Jerome* and a number of Flemish works.

Via San Pietro 29. Tel: (0577) 46052.
Open: Tue–Sat 8am–7pm, Sun–Mon
8am–1.30pm. Advance booking:
www.ticketeria.it

Walk: Siena town

This walk goes right across the city, from one gate to another. It shows just how small Siena is, for walking briskly and without stopping, you could cross the entire city in 20 minutes. Of course, you will want to take longer because of the numerous distractions along the route.

Allow 1 hour.

Start at the Porta Fontebranda.

1 Porta Fontebranda

Just outside this gate there is a good view of the city wall as it climbs the hill. The 14th-century wall still completely encircles Siena, a remarkable construction as it climbs

and dips around the crests of the hills. The Porta Fontebranda takes its name from the immense covered fountain a short way up the street. Built in the 13th century, it was so well known that Dante made reference to it in *The Divine Comedy*. Towering above it to the left is the immense basilica of San

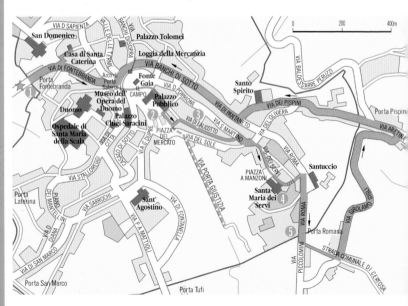

Domenico. A little further up on the left, in Via di Santa Caterina, a short flight of steps leads to the Casa di Santa Caterina, the house in which St Catherine of Siena was born.

Return to the Porta Fontebranda and, with your back to the fountain, head up Via di Fontebranda, then cross the Via de Città, pass under the Arco di Porta Salaria and enter Il Campo (see pp115–16). Keep to the right-hand side of the Campo, following the façade of the Palazzo Pubblico, and turn right, beside the Torre del Mangia, into Via di Salicotto. Take the first right, down Via di Peschieri, and so enter the Piazza del Mercato.

2 Piazza del Mercato

This square is the setting for a bustling fruit and vegetable market.

If you would like the experience of a country walk in the heart of a city, take the steps which lead down from this southern end of the Piazza del Mercato and follow Via Porta Giustizia, a narrow lane which runs along the valley. Otherwise, turn left out of Piazza del Mercato, along Via dei Malcontenti to return to Via di Salicotto, where you turn right.

3 Via di Salicotto

A few metres along you will come to a dramatic example of local patriotism, a terrace decorated with modern sculpture and the Elephant and Castle statue of the Torre (Tower) *contrada*, one of the city's ancient parishes. The *contrada* has a little museum at No 76 (ring for the custodian).

At the next road junction turn right and follow Via dei Servi, which leads to a quiet, tree-lined square fronting the church of Santa Maria dei Servi.

4 Santa Maria dei Servi

Climb the steps of this church (*open: daily 9am–noon & 3–5pm*) for a stupendous view of Siena's skyline. Santa Maria contains notable paintings such as the rather horrific *Massacre of the Innocents* by Pietro Lorenzetti.

On leaving the church, turn right and descend into a tree-lined road leading to Via Roma. Turn right here for the Porta Romana.

5 Porta Romana

Almost every Italian city has a 'Roman Gate', suggesting that all roads do, indeed, lead to Rome. This gate is a vast, roofless structure in pink brick with a marble bench all the way round. The Medici balls proclaim that Siena was once ruled by Florence.

You can either turn back here or, if you have the energy, continue on through the Porta Romana and take the road immediately to the left, the Strada Comunale di Certosa. After 100m (110yds), turn left along Via Girolamo Gigli. This runs for 400m (440yds) through a mixture of countryside and suburb roughly parallel to the city wall. It leads to the Porta Pispini where you enter the city again, following Via dei Pispini back towards the city centre.

Tour: Florence to Greve in Chianti

Starting from the turmoil of the bus station in Florence, this pleasant tour will take you along the romantically named Chiantigiana (the Chianti Way), passing through the quiet towns and villages of Chianti to Greve, one of the main towns in this little empire of wine. There are frequent bus departures from Florence to Greve (at least two an hour). This is also an attractive route for motorists and even cyclists: the distance involved is just about 30km (19 miles), though the hills are steep.

Allow 1 hour by bus.

Florence has developed relatively little to the south, so as you leave the city on the N222 you will quickly gain open country. You will pass under the A1 (the great Autostrada del Sole linking Milan to Rome, which also acts as a bypass for Florence) just before Grassina. From this point on, the N222 really does live up to its name, the Chiantigiana, as it ascends a ridge with wide views of typical Chianti landscapes on either side. For golf addicts, the manicured lawns of Ugolino, Florence's golf club, are on the right just beyond Grassina.

Strada in Chianti is the next main stop along the road. The name Strada, meaning highway, is thought to date back to the Roman era and suggests that today's N222 follows the course of a Roman road. Not far away, the immense **Castello di Mugnana** (*www. castellodimugnana.com*) stands guard over the road. This is one of the region's best preserved medieval castles; today it stands at the core of a big wine estate. If you are travelling by car or bicycle you can stop off here or at any of the other numerous *fattorie*, or wine farms, which line the route. Look out for notices on the side of the road saying '*Vendita Diretta*' – many offer free tastings, but having sampled the wine, you are expected to make a purchase.

Beyond Strada the road begins to descend rapidly towards Greve in Chianti. The pretty little town is an important centre for the prestigious Chianti wine trade. Like many of its neighbours, it holds a wine festival every September when the entire town centre takes on a festive mood. The core of the town is the splendid triangular market place, the **Piazza Matteotti**. The buildings on all three sides are fronted by colonnades: the balconies above that, in summer, are ablaze with flowers. Shaded by the colonnades there are numerous small (and rather expensive) shops; as you would expect, many specialise in the wines of the Chianti region, while others specialise in *cinghiale* (wild boar) in various forms – such as delicious hams and sausages.

In the centre of the piazza is a handsome statue of Giovanni da Verrazzano, a 16th-century explorer who is credited with being the first European to visit the North American coastline where New York would one day be built. He was born in the

Castello di Verrazzano, about 4km (2½ miles) away, which sells a wide range of wines and olive oils.

If you are travelling by car or bicycle you can continue down the N222 all the way to Siena, calling at **Castellina in Chianti** along the route. Like San Gimignano, this hilltop town owes its picturesque appearance to the bitter necessities of medieval warfare. Castellina stood on the border between Florentine and Sienese territory and controlled the junction of the region's three main roads. That accounts for its stout encircling walls, which are almost intact, together with the well-restored castle at the heart of the town, and one of its more unusual attractions – the extraordinary gallery or covered walkway called the Via delle Volte, built as part of the 15th-century defences.

Radda in Chianti, surrounded by vineyards

Versilia (Tuscan Riviera)

The Italian seaside tends to arouse strong feelings among non-Italians. Accustomed to the idea that access to the beaches and the sea is one of the few free pleasures left in the world, visitors are startled to find that this is not always the case in Italian resorts. Flying in to Pisa airport, you will have a good view of the so-called Tuscan Riviera. It stretches from Marina di Carrara in the north all the way down to Livorno, a distance of some 60km (37 miles), and nearly the whole of this seafront is lined by bathing establishments.

Most of the eight towns, including the largest, Viareggio, are strung along the long coastline called the Versilia, and located several kilometres inland from the sea – but they all have a beach area known as a marina. The layout of all marinas is identical: hotels, restaurants, cafés and shops, all set within a strict grid pattern of streets.

Beach facilities

Some parts of the beach are free, and marked 'Spiaggia Pubblica' or 'Libera'. But for the most part beaches are developed as bathing establishments called *stabilimenti,* usually a connected range of bathing cabins arranged around a central fountain or flower garden. They belong to a nearby hotel, or are operated by a commercial company. The entrance fee covers the hire of one cabin for four people and the use of umbrellas and lounge chairs. There is sure to be a bar or restaurant within arm's length.

Viareggio

On the map, Versilia towns appear to run into each other, but each has its individual core and good tourist information facilities. Viareggio is definitely the pearl of the Versilia. Its street plan displays the same relentless grid pattern, but a high proportion of the development consists of private houses with small front gardens. These, along with the tree-lined roads and squares, make up a pleasant green town.

Viareggio also has a port area where, mixed among the luxury yachts, there are tramp steamers and fishing boats. Local housewives and restaurateurs come to the port to buy their fish straight off the boat. From the end of the immensely long quay is a superb view of the whole Tuscan Riviera stretching northwards, with the Apuan Alps (Alpi Apuane) forming a majestic backdrop.

The long seafront promenade called the Viale Regina Margherita is an

Viareggio town plan

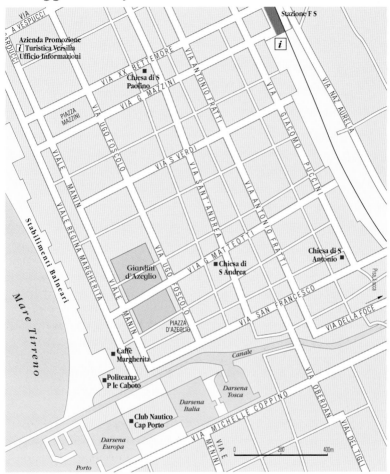

example of good town planning, for the route is broken up at regular intervals by green squares and shady trees. Towards the port area, the buildings lining this promenade break out into cheerful Art Nouveau extravaganza. Doyen of them all is the Gran Caffè Margherita, with its extraordinary cupolas covered with colourful ceramic tiles in a vaguely Persian style and a proud notice stating that Puccini frequently dined there. Viareggio is a good base for excursions. The main tourist information office at Viale Carducci 10 (*tel: (0584) 962 233; www.aptversilia.it*) provides a free guidebook entitled *Itineraries for Tourists* which details 19 tours in the area.

Volterra

This rather eerie city, situated on a windswept plateau at over 500m (1,640ft) above sea level, is one of the oldest continually inhabited cities in Italy. The Etruscans established a settlement on this natural citadel around 800 BC, and there is evidence of even earlier occupation. The Etruscan city, called Velathri, became one of the most powerful in the Dodecapolis, the 12-city alliance. Present-day Volterra occupies only about a third of the area of ancient Velathri.

One of the most interesting ways to approach the city is from the north or the east; as you climb towards Volterra you will see the towering *balze*, dramatic precipices caused by landslips that are slowly eating away at the Etruscan circuit of walls. The surrounding countryside is rich in minerals, including alum and alabaster. Alum was once the source of the city's wealth but also of its downfall, for Florence laid violent hands upon Volterra in 1361, determined to control the supply of alum, an important ingredient for dyeing cloth. Alabaster mining was revived in the 19th century and is today Volterra's major industry.

The city is full of shops selling everything from alabaster sculptures to table lamps and bowls worked in this marble-like stone.
Tourist Information Office, Via Giusto Turazza 2. Tel: (0588) 86150; www.provolterra.it

Duomo (Cathedral)

For all its modest appearance Volterra's cathedral, begun in the 13th century, contains interesting details: the great pulpit is in Pisan Romanesque style, while the chapel in the right-hand (south) transept has a startling 13th-century *Deposition* carved in wood.
Piazza del Duomo. Open: daily 8am–1pm & 4–7pm. Free admission.

Museo Etrusco Guarnacci (Etruscan Museum)

This is one of the most important museums of Etruscan art in Italy. The collection consists of more than 600 funerary urns designed to hold cremated remains and made of carved alabaster, travertine or terracotta. The urns were all unearthed from ancient Etruscan cemeteries around the city.

The bas-reliefs on the urns tell us a great deal about Etruscan life and beliefs. One of the most famous urns is the so-called *Urna degli Sposi* (the Married

Couple Urn). It is a startling example of realistic portraiture, depicting the rather coarse-featured couple 'warts and all'. Equally renowned is the mysterious, elongated bronze figure known as *Ombra della Sera* ('Shadow of the Night'), discovered in 1879 and used as a fire-poker until experts realised this was a masterpiece of Etruscan art.

Via Don Minzoni 15. Tel: (0588) 86347. Open: daily 16 Mar–Oct 9am–7pm; Nov–15 Mar 9am–2pm. Last entry: 15 minutes before closing time. Admission charge.

Parco Archeologico

This small park occupies the site of the ancient Etruscan acropolis, and dotted around the grounds are the remains of temple foundations and Roman cisterns. Towering over the park is the Fortezza Medicea, a well-preserved fortress (1492) still used as a prison.

Via di Castello. Open: daily Mar–Nov 10.30am–5.30pm; Nov–Mar Sat & Sun 10am–4pm. Admission charge.

Piazza dei Priori

This characterful square stands at the heart of the medieval city. Its centrepiece, the Palazzo dei Priori, is probably the oldest town hall in Tuscany. Begun in 1208, it established the pattern followed by Florence.

Opposite is the 13th-century Palazzo Pretorio with its cheerful Torre del Porcellino (Piglet's Tower), taking its name from the little piglet carved on the base.

On the right-hand side of the square is the showroom of the local alabaster-carving co-operative, displaying the work of Volterra's artists.

Pinacoteca (Art Gallery)

This splendid new gallery opened in 1992 and is housed in a 15th-century palazzo designed by Antonio da Sangallo the Elder. The collection is small but contains several outstanding works, most notably Rosso Fiorentino's *Deposition* (1521), a dramatic example of Mannerist painting renowned for its bold colouring.

Via dei Sarti 2. Tel: (0588) 87580. Open: daily 16 Mar–Oct 9am–7pm; Nov–15 Mar 9am–2pm. Admission charge.

Porta all'Arco

The actual arch is a Roman reconstruction, but the lower courses of massive stone without mortar are pure Etruscan. So too are the three blackened heads over the arch.

Teatro Romano (Roman Theatre)

Volterra's Roman theatre and baths lie just outside the walls to the north of the city. The theatre, which is still being excavated, is the best preserved in Tuscany. The best views are to be had from Via Lunga le Mura which follows the line of the medieval walls.

Piazza Caduti Martiri dei Lager Nazisti. Tel: (800) 22 33 00. Open: daily mid-Mar–early Nov 10.30am–5.30pm; early Nov–mid-Mar Sat & Sun 10am–4pm. Admission charge.

Hill villages

Roman cities in Tuscany are nearly always located in the valleys and plains, but the ancient Etruscans and their medieval descendants preferred to build on hill tops where the chance of fending off an enemy attack was that much greater. The Tuscan landscape is dotted with such hilltop towns, many of them of great age. Here are some examples of the most characterful.

Artimino

Originally an Etruscan town, Artimino is now a tranquil walled village (22km/14 miles west of Florence) with a population of fewer than 300. It offers superb views over the Tuscan countryside, and on summer nights fireflies and nightingales make it an enchanted spot. Some of the stone used to build the 12th-century church of San Leonardo came from the nearby Etruscan cemetery of Pian di Rosello (look for road signs pointing to the cemetery, site of archaeological excavations). Just above the town is a 16th-century Medici villa, originally built as a hunting lodge by Buontalenti for Duke Ferdinand I. It is known as the 'Villa of a Hundred Chimneys' because of its bristling roofline. A luxury hotel and restaurant adjoin the villa's grounds.

Montefioralle

This silent, inward-looking village, 1.5km (1 mile) west of Greve in Chianti, resembles one great castle, so closely integrated are its tower houses, its encircling wall and its Romanesque churches.

Monteriggioni

Dante compared the giants who surround the ninth circle of hell in his *Inferno* to the 14 towers that still surround this perfect little walled village (located 15km/9 miles northwest of Siena). The wall and towers were built in the early 13th century by Siena as a frontier post on the border between its territory and that of its larger northern enemy, Florence, and are some of the best preserved in Italy.

Exploring Monteriggioni's tiny interior, you become aware of the reason why the Italians tend to call every settlement larger than a hamlet a *città* (city); with its two proud piazzas and its Romanesque church, this really does feel less like a village and more like a city in miniature.

Typical Tuscan hilltop town

Getting away from it all

*'There are thousands, millions of utterly
secluded little nooks, though the land
has been under cultivation these
thousands of years.'*

E M FORSTER

A Room with a View, 1908

GARDENS

The Renaissance formal garden almost invariably attached to a rural villa was designed as an outdoor extension of the house, with staircases, avenues and 'rooms' delineated in box hedging. In time, gardens became ever more elaborate, decorated with statuary, grottoes, fountains and *giochi d'acqua* ('water games') – hidden jets which drenched the unsuspecting visitor. The following are some of the best examples of Renaissance gardens to be seen in Tuscany.

Giardino di Boboli
(Boboli Gardens), Florence

The Boboli Gardens were designed as an extension of the Pitti Palace (*see pp59–61*) and they were laid out from 1549, with additional details added over the next 60 years. Since the Pitti Palace was the home of Tuscany's 'royal family', Grand Duke Cosimo I and his wife Eleonora, the gardens were designed to show their power and splendour. In 1589, for example, to celebrate the marriage of their son, Ferdinando, the palace courtyard was flooded to create the setting for a mock naval battle using 18 galleons. The main flight of steps leading up through the garden brings you to an immense pool and statue of Neptune. The avenue of cypresses which descends from here leads to a charming water garden, the Isolotto.

Piazza dei Pitti. Tel: (055) 213 440/318 741); www.firenzemusei.it. Open: daily from 8.15am all year (until 4.30pm Nov–Feb, 5.30pm Mar, 6.30pm Apr–May & Sept–Oct, 7.30pm June–Aug). Closed: first & last Mon each month. Admission charge. Advance booking tel: (055) 294 083.

Palazzo Piccolomini
(Piccolomini Palace), Pienza

In 1459 Pius II decided to turn Corsignano, the village in which he was born, into a model town. Pienza is the result. In the main square of the tiny

hilltop town, Pius II built himself a palace, the Palazzo Piccolomini, and behind this palace is what can only be described as a 'hanging garden'. The garden is not very large, but its designer, Bernardo Rossellino, took full advantage of the dramatic site, a narrow shelf between the palace and the very edge of the steep hillside.
Piazza Pio II. Tel: (0578) 748 350; www.palazzopiccolominipienza.it. Open: Tue–Sun 10am–6.30pm (mid-Oct–mid-Mar 4.30pm). Admission charge.

Villa Garzoni, Collodi

The Garzoni family bought the old castle of Collodi (15km/9 miles east of Lucca) in the early 17th century and converted it into a magnificent villa. The garden was laid out in the Baroque style in 1786 and is a famous example of the last, luscious flowering of the formal garden before the fashion for naturalistic landscape gardening took over. The

The theatrical gardens of the Villa Garzoni

garden is, in effect, an enormous stage set with its statuary, fountains, topiary and a dramatic series of staircase terraces cascading down the hillside away from the villa at its summit.
Tel: (0572) 429 590. Open: daily summer 8am–sunset, winter 8am–4.30pm. Admission charge.

Villa Medicea la Petraia and Villa Medicea di Castello

These two Medici villas in the northwestern suburbs of Florence stand almost next to each other and are easily reached by bus Nos 28a, b or c; buses leave every 15 minutes or so from the main bus station. The journey takes about 15 minutes. Get off at Frazione Castello, as close as possible to Villa Medicea la Petraia, off Via Reginaldo Giuliani. Via Medicea la Petraia leads up to the 16th-century Villa Medicea la Petraia whose gardens are laid out with box hedges in geometric patterns enclosing flower beds. You can also wander through extensive wild woodland at the rear of the villa.

Its close neighbour, the Villa Medicea di Castello, is well signposted. The garden was laid out for Cosimo I in 1541 and features a shell-encrusted grotto for which Giambologna made the naturalistic bronze birds now displayed in the Bargello (*see pp56–8*). *Frazione Castello. Tel: (055) 454 791. Both gardens open: daily 8.15am–dusk. Di Castello closed 2nd & 3rd Mon of month. Free admission. Advance booking tel: (055) 294 883.*

SPAS

An Italian characteristic, which has endured down the centuries, is the obsession with bathing and other forms of water therapy. The Romans were, of course, very fond of their baths and built them in every part of the world that they conquered, even at the chilly extremes of their empire.

The descendants of the Romans have continued the tradition, using the same word *terme* for the institution (the word 'spa', derived from the name of a town in Belgium, is never used in Italy).

The *terme* performs two separate but related functions. First, there is the therapeutic. Italy has no higher number of hypochondriacs than any other country but the advertisements for the *terme* do suggest a rather gruesome preoccupation with disorders of the liver, bowels and bladder. Water cures are taken under medical supervision and range from immersion and steam inhalations to simple consumption of measured doses of mineral-rich aqueous liquid. The other function of the *terme* is to supply relaxation and entertainment. Drinking water that tastes of sulphur and iron filings is not one of the greatest of gastronomic experiences, and the promoters have gone to great trouble to create various distractions, ranging from concerts to sports, all of which take place in beautiful surroundings. Tuscany is particularly well provided with *terme*, the following being the most popular.

Bagni di Lucca

Situated about 25km (15½ miles) north of Lucca, this is said to be the oldest *terme* in continual use in Italy, on the strength that Countess Matilda, the 11th-century ruler of northern Tuscany, is known to have bathed in the town's warm springs. The *terme* is located in beautiful wooded countryside, set among hills along the rushing River Lima. It achieved its social prominence in the early 19th century when Napoleon's sister, Elisa Baciocchi, briefly the ruler of Lucca, presided over a glittering social world. Distinguished foreign visitors to Bagni di Lucca have included Montaigne, Byron, Heine and Shelley. Europe's first licensed casino opened here in 1837; the original building has been fully restored. *www.termebagnidilucca.it*

Chianciano Terme

The ancient Etruscans made use of these hot springs, but the mineral-rich waters have only been exploited on a large scale since the 1940s. Unlike Bagni

Hot springs occur naturally at Saturnia, in southern Tuscany

Barga and the Garfagnana

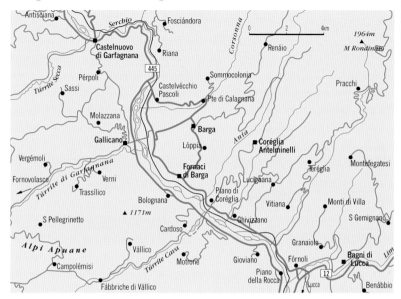

di Lucca, which still retains the atmosphere of the past, Chianciano is functional and crisply modern.

It does, however, have the attraction of the historic old town of Chianciano just 2km (1 mile) from the *terme*, and there are several historic hilltop towns in the immediate vicinity, such as Montepulciano (*see pp102–3*) and Chiusi (*see p85*).

Montecatini Terme

This is the most upmarket Tuscan *terme*, famous throughout Italy for its varied architecture and fine gardens. Montecatini is a bustling modern city on the main railway line between Lucca and Florence, while the Parco delle Terme, the site of the spa, forms a large green wedge to the north of the city.

Dotted around the green lawns of the Parco are nine separate thermal establishments, each built over a spring. The oldest is the Tettuccio, known since at least the 14th century but not developed until the 18th century. Its architecture is also the most distinguished. A day ticket is expensive, but for this you can drink and bathe in the warm, salty waters in the most luxurious surroundings.
www.termemontecatini.it

BARGA AND THE GARFAGNANA

Variety in the landscape is one of the great attractions of Tuscany. The Lucca plain, along with the Arno Valley to the south, is flat and densely developed, yet just a few kilometres to the north, you enter a totally different landscape of towering peaks, narrow valleys cloaked in woodland, and tumbling rivers icy cold from melting snow. The River Serchio, along with its tributaries, the Lima and the Secca, have, over the millennia, cut a course through the high mountains that form the central feature of the region. Major roads follow these main valleys, but once you depart from the beaten track you will find a wild landscape with peaks dotted with tiny, ancient villages.

In recent years, parts of the Garfagnana have been designated as a nature reserve, or Parco Naturale, while others have begun to be developed for sports such as hang-gliding and skiing. There are also many hiking trails and the landscape is so varied that at one extreme it offers gentle strolls through meadows and woodlands, while at the other the conditions would test a mountaineer. To explore the region you really do need to have your own transport. There is a railway line that follows the Serchio valley from Lucca to Aulla, but the mountainous nature of the region means that some stations – Barga and Bagni di Lucca in particular – are a considerable way from the town itself. The LAZZI buses from Lucca will take you to Barga within an hour, and Castelnuovo in about an hour and a half.

Barga

The little town of Barga sits on a hill over 400m (1,300ft) above sea level, and the terrace in front of the cathedral at the highest point in the town offers an exhilarating vista to the high peaks of the Alpi Apuane range. One can only marvel at the stubborness of the inhabitants who built their imposing cathedral in the 9th century on this dizzying spot. There are splendid Romanesque carvings round the outside of the cathedral, and the great tank of a pulpit, dating from the 13th century, is carved with scenes from the life of Christ. There is a small archaeological museum to the north of the church, while the rest of the town winds and twists down the hillside.

Castelnuovo di Garfagnana

Perched at the confluence of the rivers Serchio and Secca, this friendly little mountain town is also a major centre for mountain sports. Trekking, mountain bike rallies, horse riding and hiking are all popular here. Although livelier than Barga, this is still a peaceful mountain town.

Information centres specialising in adventure holidays: APT Castelnuovo di Garfagnana, Via Cavalieri Vittorio Veneto, tel: (0583) 644 354; Cooperativa Garfagnana Vacanze, Piazza delle Erbe, tel: (0583) 65169.

Grotta del Vento (Cave of the Wind)

The Cave of the Wind, near Fornovolasco, 9km (6 miles) southwest of Barga, is part of a massive cave system located deep within the mountains of the Apuan Alps. Visitors are taken on guided tours, ranging between one and three hours.

Tel (to check if open): (0583) 722 020; www.grottadelvento.com. Open: daily 10am–6pm. Admission charge. Take along warm clothing – the depths of this cave system are always icily cold.

PARCO NATURALE DELLA MAREMMA

Designated as a nature reserve in June 1975, this great park stretches for some 20km (12½ miles) northwards from the little fishing village of Talamone. Protection does not mean that the park area has become fossilised: rural industries still continue to thrive within it, but hunting is forbidden and cars are not allowed.

The relative difficulty of access is part of the park's attraction, for it is rarely crowded and the varied vegetation supports many different kinds of wildlife. From the end of the Roman era, when neglect led to the choking up of the region's drainage systems, the Maremma was a place to be avoided, its stagnant marshes a breeding ground for malarial mosquitoes. The locality did not even have a proper name; *maremma* simply means 'land by the sea'. Re-draining and re-colonisation of the marshes began in the 18th century under Grand Duke Pietro Leopoldo, but the northern area of the park retains a number of undrained lagoons which can be explored by canoe and where the birdlife is very rich.

The unploughed Maremma pasture is grazed by cattle. They are herded by horse-borne *butteri*, Italy's own version of the cowboy, so skilled at their task

that in the 19th century they actually competed in rodeos and defeated the legendary Buffalo Bill Cody and his team. Every August, American cowboys compete with the *butteri* in special shows put on in Alberese.

For those who want to explore the park in more detail, there are four waymarked trails (a map is provided when you buy your entrance permit). On the other hand, you may decide just to laze on the beaches, which are among the most attractive in Tuscany.

For restaurants and hotels, the little walled fishing village of Talamone at the southern tip of the park is ideal, and there is a huge choice of places to stay and eat at further south in Orbetello. *It is not easy to get to the park without private transport. Six trains run daily from Siena to Grosseto, the nearest big city. Buses run on an irregular basis to Alberese, the park's headquarters. For timings, check with either the Grosseto Tourist Office at Viale Monterosa 206 (tel: (0564) 462 611; www.lamaremmafabene.it. Open: Mon–Sat 8am–2pm), or the park headquarters in Alberese (tel: (0564) 407 098; www.parco-maremma.it). Park hours are deliberately restrictive: officially you can enter at 9am, and stay until 1 hour before sunset, on Wed, Sat, Sun & bank holidays. Buy entry permits from the ticket office in Alberese. Fee includes bus transportation (hourly; last bus out at 5.30pm) to Marina di Alberese, a stretch of fine beach, sheltered by umbrella pines, with picnic facilities.*

Shopping

The regional pattern of Italian society, along with sturdily conservative traditions, come out clearly in manufacturing and retailing. Almost every town specialises in some locally manufactured product, whether it is ceramics in Siena or alabaster in Volterra. Even cosmopolitan Florence, which has international names such as Gucci, Valentino and Ferragamo side by side on the Via de'Tornabuoni, is as proud as any village of its leather products, made in the backstreet workshops of Santo Spirito and San Frediano.

Tuscany has few supermarkets; small shops are the norm and retailers usually have a direct link with manufacturers – which in their turn are frequently small enterprises. Thus the Italian tradition of individual craftsmanship not only survives, it flourishes, and the quality is very high – although caution must be exercised when dealing with street traders. They react with amazing rapidity to new demands; stalls selling umbrellas will sprout up within minutes of the start of any downpour, but the umbrellas they sell will not last out the week.

The high quality of most products means that goods are not cheap. Haggling is definitely not an Italian custom, but as the person serving you is very probably the owner of the shop (and possibly related to the manufacturer) and so can make on-the-spot decisions, there is a certain flexibility in pricing. It does not hurt to ask for a discount (*sconto*) particularly

if you are spending a lot of money with that shop.

Shopping hours

In general, shop opening hours are 9am–1pm, and 3.30/4pm to 7/8pm, although the bigger shops in Florence and other big cities have now started experimenting with all-day opening. Shops tend to put their shutters up earlier on Saturday afternoon (around 5/5.30pm) and many do not open on Monday morning. Very few shops open on Sunday. Most shops also close for one day or half a day a week in addition to Sunday – details of the closing day will be posted on the door. In big cities, such as Florence, Lucca, Pisa or Siena, there will be one late shopping night a week, often Thursday.

Value Added Tax

Tourists from countries outside the European Union can claim a rebate of IVA (the Italian version of Value Added

Tax) on individual purchases in excess of €155. Stores that participate in this scheme will supply full details and provide you with the necessary documentation.

FLORENCE

Although Florence is overshadowed as a shopping centre by Milan and Rome, when it comes to pride in quality craftsmanship the city is still in a class on its own. If you want to see craftsmen at work, simply wander round Piazza Santa Spirito or any of the other narrow streets of the Oltrarno, the part of Florence that stands on the south side of the river.

Antiques

The problem that faces the innocent abroad in Florence looking for antiques and works of art is well illustrated by the superb advertisement put out by the **Galleria Frilli** (*Via dei Fossi 26r*), who specialises in both genuine antiques and reproductions in marble and bronze: it is nothing less than a full-scale replica of Ghiberti's Baptistery doors. Renaissance Florence was, after all, the place which invented the *bottega* (workshop) system whereby the master would outline the project but leave much of the details to his apprentices. The borderline between work of art and copy, between genuine and reproduction is not always clear, so if you are not an antiques expert, be wary of parting with large amounts of money.

Art paper

Giulio Giannini e Figlio (*Piazza Pitti 37r; www.giuliogiannini.it*) makes and sells the marbled paper which has been a speciality of Florence for at least six centuries. **Parione** (*Via del Parione 10r; www.parione.it*) prides itself on selling 'the kind of paper you would expect to find in Michelangelo's home town'.

Beauty products

Florentine herbs and flowers are used in the famous handmade beauty products and remedies of the **Oficina Profumo Farmaceutica di Santa Maria Novella**, believed to be the oldest pharmacy in the world. Still fashioned in the traditional methods created by the Dominican brothers, the simple wares (complete with 19th-century-style

Enticing antiques from near and far

packaging) are sold from the former church of the original 13th-century friary.
Via della Scale 16. Tel: (055) 216 276; www.smnovella.it

Books and prints

Florence maintains its link with scholarship through a marvellous range of bookshops. For visitors who do not read Italian, the simply named **BM Bookshop** (*corner of Via Borgognissanti & Piazza Goldoni; www. bmbookshop.com*) is indispensable for its range of guidebooks and local histories in various languages, but principally English. **Feltrinelli** (*Via Cavour 12–20r; www.lafeltrinelli.it*) also has an excellent foreign-language section.

Clothing

The upmarket shops are concentrated in Via de' Tornabuoni. **Gucci** still

Vini e salumi – wines and sausages

remains loyal to its roots at Via de' Tornabuoni 73r, and **Salvatore Ferragamo** is firmly entrenched in the splendid Palazzo Spini-Feroni 16r. **Armani** can be found at 48/50r.

Designer outlets

The **Mall** (*Via Europa 8. Leccio/Reggello. Tel: (055) 865 7755. Open: daily 10am–7pm*) outlet store stocks discounted Gucci, Giorgio Armani, Yves Saint Laurent and Bottega Veneto products. **Il Pellettieri d'Italia** (*Località Levanella. Montevarchi. Tel: (055) 91901. Open: daily at 9.30am*) offers reductions on Prada items. It's hard to find but well worth the hunt. Arrive early for the best bargains. If you're without a car, many tour operators offer day trips to fashion outlets.

Jewellery

Ever since Ferdinando I expelled the butchers, blacksmiths and tanners from the Ponte Vecchio in 1593, the bridge has been famous for its jewellers' shops. Do not be misled by the modest-looking shopfronts: the goods sold here can be expensive (although you can also buy very modestly priced trinkets). At least you know that the goods sold in these shops as gold really are gold – unlike the 'genuine gold jewellery' sold at remarkably low prices by peddlers on the bridge. Away from the Ponte Vecchio you may find the prices less hyped. **Ugo Piccini** has an elegant shop (*base of a tower at Via Por Santa Maria*

9–11r; www.ugopiccini.it) which
specialises in watches and jewellery.

Leather

Leather goods are sold virtually
everywhere in Florence, from the stalls
in Piazza San Lorenzo market, where
identical belts are hung in their
hundreds (cheap but good) to the
elegance of the **Bottega Fiorentina**
(*Borgo de'Greci 5; www.
bottegafiorentina.it*). The latter is set in
a palazzo with a delightful courtyard
and fountain.

OUTSIDE FLORENCE
Arezzo

The Piazza Grande is a good place to
shop for antiques and reproductions.
The entire piazza is given over to an
antiques fair on the first Sunday of
every month.

Montepulciano

The **Azienda Agraria** (*Via San Donato*)
is a farm co-operative selling honey and
wax products (including soap made
from honey) and the knee-buckling
liqueur called Aquavita di
Montepulciano. Nearby, **Ramela
Mazzetti** (*Via San Donato 15a*) sells
copper utensils, new and antique.

Pietrasanta

Pietrasanta (the name literally means
'Holy Stone') is located on the coast,
18km (11 miles) south of Carrara, and
appropriately enough specialises in
marble goods. Packed with artisan

workshops and artists' studios, this
city has been an important centre for
artistic sculpture since Michelangelo's
day. Some of the marble workshops
and bronze foundries are open to the
public, and shops and galleries are
full of locally manufactured marble
goods, ceramics, mosaics and items
in terracotta.

Siena

Sena Vetus: Antichità (*Via di Città 53*)
is an antique shop which tempts you to
come in and browse among the artfully
casual display. For books, the nearby
Libreria Senese (*Via di Città 66,
tel: (0577) 280 845*) stocks everything
from scholarly monographs to science
fiction in several foreign languages as
well as Italian; the shop is also excellent
for local maps and guides. The shop
extends on to a mezzanine gallery – and
this gallery carries a stunning range of
books for children.

For ceramics, one of Siena's
specialities, try **Neri: Ceramiche Santa
Caterina** (*Via di Città 51, tel: (0577)
283 098*). This has a glittering display of
traditional designs and there is usually
someone in the shop working on a
design, bearing out the proudly
displayed claim '*Produzione Propria*'
(handmade).

Another fascinating shop in the
same street is **Stampe Cornici Bianchi**
(*Via di Città 112*) which sells historic
and modern posters, with a particularly
interesting range illustrating the Palio
(*see pp148–9*).

Markets

Every day in summer the little town of Pescia, some 27km (17 miles) east of Lucca, bursts into multi-coloured bloom. This is Italy's largest flower market, with over 1,000 growers selling millions of flowers to hundreds of florists from all over Europe. Many of these flowers are grown in the surrounding countryside, and the fields either side of the N435, between Lucca and Pescia, are a patchwork quilt of colourful flowers.

In Arezzo, the Piazza Grande is taken over on the first Sunday of every month by a popular antiques fair. The products displayed on some stalls may challenge your idea of what constitutes an antique, but it is nevertheless fun to browse and occasionally take a gamble.

In Siena, the feast of Santa Lucia in December is marked with a massive display of ceramics, one of the city's major art forms.

Local produce on sale at a market in Siena

Florence boasts five general markets. The biggest is the Tuesday-morning market in the Cascine Park, to the west of the city, where Florentines buy bargain-priced clothes and shoes. Another market takes over Piazza San Lorenzo, alongside San Lorenzo Church, every day in the summer and every day except Sunday and Monday in winter. You can buy excellent leather goods here – and some designer-label accessories at suspiciously low prices. Adjoining the piazza is the covered Mercato Centrale, a 19th-century architectural gem in its own right. The market is crowded with food stalls and closes at 2pm.

The Mercato Nuovo (despite its name, the 'New Market' was founded in the 16th century) stands just to the west of the Piazza della Signoria; its appeal is unabashedly touristic and it specialises in souvenirs. There is also a small daily flea market in the Piazza dei Ciompi in the east of the city; mainly junk and second-hand goods, but authentic antique dealers also trade there. Not far from the flea market is the lively Mercato San Ambrogio, in Piazza San Ambrogio. It is a good place to pick up typical Tuscan products, at non-tourist prices.

Oils and pastas at Florence's Central Market

Entertainment

Big cities such as Florence, Siena and Pisa offer the best chance of enjoying professional entertainment. The student populations of these cities also ensure that there is plenty of nightlife, although fashions change with bewildering rapidity. Even in these big cities, however, Tuscans largely seek out the traditional and spontaneous forms of entertainment provided by human contact.

The evening promenade, a leisurely meal with friends in a favourite restaurant, conversation over a glass of wine in a café, or simply watching the world go by in the main piazza: it is no accident that many an Italian square resembles a theatrical stage on which the comedy of human manners is played out nightly.

The Italian passion for music (and especially opera) is a boon for non-Italian-speaking visitors. Even in the smallest cities there is bound to be a concert on somewhere during the week. In Florence, the major festival of classical music, opera and ballet, called the Maggio Musicale Fiorentino, runs from late April to early July. Lucca puts on an ambitious opera season in the autumn, usually featuring one or more operas by Puccini, who was born in the city (*see p93*). Opera is to Italy what ballet is to Russia, and, apart from the superb music, it is staged with enormous panache. It does, however, tend to be rather expensive.

Film is also extremely popular, and every town has at least one cinema. In summer, films are also shown in the open air. Though Hollywood productions tend to dominate the cinema screens, almost all films are dubbed into Italian. However, some theatres and cinema clubs in the larger cities offer original-language films on selected nights of the week.

Listings information can be found in the regionally based daily newspaper, *La Nazione* (*www.lanazione.it*). Though published in Florence, this carries local inserts for each of the nine provinces in Tuscany, including news of local events. The very useful English-language publication, *Florence: Concierge Information* (*www.florence-concierge.it*), is available free at most hotels. *Firenze Spettacolo* (*www.firenzespettacolo.it*) is published monthly in Italian and is available at most newspaper stands and bookshops. The tourist boards of Siena and Pisa publish an annual calendar of events which is available free from the tourist offices. Siena also has a lively weekly arts publication, *La Voce del Campo*. The *Florentine* (*www.theflorentine.net*) is a bi-weekly newspaper published in English with news and listings.

In recent years, partly in response to tourist demand and partly out of a traditional love of spectacle, Florence has evolved a remarkable series of spontaneous street theatres. After the evening stroll, *passeggiata*, the **Piazza della Signoria**, the **Piazza del Duomo** and the street that links the two, **Via dei Calzaiuoli**, become a continuous stage occupied by different groups. Mime artists take over **Piazza della Signoria** and are watched by crowds of around 100 or more.

Via dei Calzaiuoli is lined with fortune-tellers using computers and printers to give a high-tech gloss to their traditional methods. Musicians, both classical and pop, play to moderate-sized audiences in the Piazza del Duomo.

Enjoy a picnic in the gorgeous Tuscan countryside

Entertainment

FLORENCE
Cafés, bars and discos

Andromeda
Via dei Cimatori 13.
Tel: (055) 292 002.
Closed: Sun.

Cabiria
Piazza Santo Spirito 4r.
Tel: (055) 215 732.
Open 8am–1am.
Closed: Tue.

Caffè La Torre
Lungarno Cellini 65r.
Open: 7.30pm–4am.

Caffè Pitti
Popular café/bar and restaurant.
Piazza Pitti 9. Tel: (055) 239 9863;
www.caffepitti.it. Open: Tue–Sun 10am–midnight.

Capocaccia
Lungarno Corsini 12/14r.
Tel: (055) 210 751.
Closed: Mon night.

Central Park
Dance club.
Via Fosso Macinante 1.
Tel: (055) 353 505.
Open: Tue–Sat 10pm until late.

Chequers Pub
Via della Scala 7/9r.
Tel: (055) 287 588.
Open: 6pm–2.30am.

Dolce Vita
Piazza del Carmine 6r.
Tel: (055) 284 595.

Enoteca Fuori Porta
Traditional wine bar.
Via Monte alle Croci 10r.
Tel: (055) 234 2483;
www.fuoriporta.it.
Open: daily 2.30pm–2am.

Jazz Club
Live music and cocktails.
Via Nuova de'Caccini 3.
Tel: (055) 247 9700;
www.jazzclubfirenze.com.
Open: 9.30pm until late.
Closed: Mon.

Maracana
Brazilian restaurant/nightclub.
Via Faenza 4a/b.
Tel: (055) 210 298;
www.maracana.it.
Closed: Mon, Tue.

Rex Cafe
Aperitifs, cocktails.
Via Fiesolana 23r.
Tel: (055) 248 0331.
www.rexcafe.it.
Open: 5pm–2.30am.
Closed: July–Aug.

Tenax
Live music and shows.
Via Pratese 46.
Tel: (055) 308 160;
www.tenax.org.
Closed: Mon.

Universale Firenze
Huge restaurant/club.
Via Pisana 77r. Tel: (055) 221 122;
www.universalefirenze.it.
Open: 7pm–3am.

Yab
Restaurant, dance club.
Via Sassetti 5r.
Tel: (055) 215 160;
www.yab.it.
Closed: Sun.

Cinemas
Atelier Alfieri
Via dell'Ulivo 6.
Tel: (055) 240 720.

Fulgor
Maso Finguerra 24r.
Tel: (055) 238 1881;
www.staseraalcinema.it/cinemafulgor

Odeon Original Sound
Via Sassetti 1.
Tel: (055) 214 068;
www.cinehall.it.

Open-air cinemas
Arena Campo di Marte
Viale Paoli.
Tel: (055) 678 841.

Arena Cinema Castello
Via Reginaldo Giuliani 374. Tel: (055) 451 480.

Arena Esterno Notte Poggetto
Via M Mercati 24/b.
Tel: (055) 481 285.

Chiardiluna
Via Monteoliveto 1.
Tel: (055) 233 7042.

Music and theatre
Amici della Musica
Via Pier Capponi 41.

Tel: (055) 608 420;
www.amicamusica.fi.it
Musicus Concentus
Piazza del Carmine 19.
Tel: (055) 287 347;
www.musicusconcentus.it
Teatro Comunale
Corso Italia 16.
Tel: (055) 277 91; www.
maggiofiorentino.com
Teatro della Pergola
Via della Pergola 18.
Tel: (055) 226 4316.
Teatro Verdi
Via Ghibellina 99.
Tel: (055) 212 320; www.
teatroverdifirenze.it

PISA AND VICINITY
Cafés, bars and
discos
Akua Keta
Via Sancasciani 8, Pisa.
Tel: (050) 43285.
Caffetteria delle
Vettovaglie
Piazza delle Vettovaglie,
Pisa. Tel: (050) 580 836.
Di là d'Arno
Via Mazzini 70, Pisa.
Tel: (050) 49449.
Lo Spaventapasseri
Via la Nunziatina 10,
Pisa. Tel: (050) 44067.
Op Art Café
Trendy wine bar.
Via San Francesco;
www.opartcafe.it. Open:
7pm–1am. Closed: Tue.

Piccadilly Pub
Lungarno Riviera,
Tirrenia.
Tel: (050) 33130.
Sweet & Sour
1970s cocktail bar.
Lungarno Mediceo 52.
Tel: (333) 37 1921. Open:
6pm–2am. Closed: Tue.
The Happy Drinker Pub
Via dei Poschi 11, Pisa.
Tel: (050) 578 555.

Cinemas
Ariston
Via Turati 27.
Tel: (050) 43407.
Arno
Via Conte Fazio.
Tel: (050) 43289.
Cinema Nuovo
Piazza delle Stazione.
Tel: (050) 41332.
Lanteri
Via San Michele degli
Scalzi 46.
Tel: (050) 577 100.
Multisala Odeon
Piazza San Paolo all'Orto.
Tel: (050) 540 168.

Music and theatre
Teatro del Giglio
Piazza del Giglio, Lucca.
Tel: (0583) 467 521;
www.teatrodelgiglio.it
Teatro Verdi
Organises programmes
at historic sites.

Via Palestro 40, Pisa.
Tel: (050) 941 111;
www.teatrodipisa.it

SIENA AND VICINITY
Cafés, bars and discos
Al Cambio
Via Pantaneto 48.
Tel: (0577) 43183.
Barone Rosso
Via Termini 9.
Tel: (0577) 286 686;
www.barone-rosso.com
L'Officina
Piazza del Sale 3.
Tel: (0577) 286 301.

Cinemas
Alessandro VII
Piazza dell'Abbadia 6.
Tel: (0577) 283 044.
Fiamma
Via Pantaneto 141.
Tel: (0577) 284 503.
Impero
Viale Vittorio
Emanuele II 14.
Tel: (0577) 48260.
Nuovo Pendola
Via San Quirico 13.
Tel: (0577) 43012; www.
cinemanuovopendola.it

Music and theatre
Accademia Musicale
Chigiana
Via di Città 89.
Tel: (0577) 22091;
www.chigiana.it

Entertainment

The Sienese Palio

The Palio is a bareback horse race run in Siena every year on 2 July and 16 August in which the prize is a *pallium* or banner. The race has been run, practically without a break, at least since the 13th century. Originally it took the form of a wild helter-skelter gallop through the city, but in the 16th century the race was transferred to the city's main square, the Piazza del Campo (*see pp115–16*). The race is still hazardous, for although the pavement of the piazza is sanded and buffers are placed between the course and the crowds of spectators, the circuit involves negotiating the steep slope of the piazza and its acute angles.

The dangers to horse and rider merely add to the thrill of the most spectacular of all Tuscany's traditional festivities, which most vividly presents the strong Tuscan sense of local patriotism. The race is run by representatives of 10 out of the 17 *contrade* or parishes of Siena. Seven of the 10 consist of those who did not compete in the previous Palio, while the other three are drawn by lot. The horses, too, are allocated to the riders by drawing lots, and it is

The Palio, a bareback horse race, is run every year in Siena

The Palio is a celebration of local patriotism

the horse, not the rider, that is most important. Under the strange (some would say nonexistent) rules, it is quite possible for a riderless horse to win the race if it shows sufficient flair in the process.

After the lots have been drawn, representatives of the *contrade* lead their horses away, keeping them under close guard, knowing that their rivals will attempt to nobble the horse. Six trial races are run before the Palio itself. This takes place in the evening and is preceded by a stirring ceremonial display put on by the *contrade*. The riders, along with many of their wildly enthusiastic supporters,

all dress in medieval costumes, featuring the colours of their *contrada*. Onlookers crowd the centre of the square, as well as the windows, balconies and roofs of the surrounding buildings, and it is certainly no place for those who are claustrophobic.

After a year's preparation, the whole race is over in about 90 seconds, the time it takes to make three circuits of the piazza. The inhabitants of the winning *contrada*, delirious with delight, then embark on a round of celebrations which can continue for weeks.
www.ilpalio.org

Children

The fact that Italians adore children, and – given the opportunity – spoil them outrageously, goes a long way towards making a family holiday in Italy a happy experience. There is no need to worry whether or not you are allowed to bring your child into a café or bar: it is assumed that a parent naturally knows best when and where to take a child.

Even in large cities, local children follow the lead set by their parents and use the city's streets and squares as a playground and stage – drawing in visiting children to join them. It is fascinating to see how rapidly small children, without a word of each other's language, are able to establish a dialogue based on mutual curiosity. The very attractions which draw their parents to Tuscany, however – the works of art, the architecture, the bustling cities – can be purgatory for the young. For them, the prime attraction of Tuscany will probably be the seaside, and, happily, the Versilia coast (*see pp126–7*) which is, in effect, one vast and safe playground.

Florence

A number of entertainments are specifically geared to children aged 6 to 14. The **Bottega dei Ragazzi** is a safe place to play that offers toys, games and books for children to use on the premises.

Piazza Santissima Annunziata 13. Tel: (055) 247 8386; www.istitutodegliinnocenti.it. Open: Mon–Sat 9am–1pm, 3–7pm.

Children can jump, bounce and climb to their hearts' content at **MondoBimbo**, an indoor recreation centre with small rides, slides, tubes and the ever-popular ball pit.

Piazza della Liberta. Tel: (055) 553 2946. Open: daily 10am–8pm (to midnight in summer). Admission charge.

On a more cultural note, the **Museo dei Ragazzi** at Palazzo Vecchio brings the Renaissance down to size with entertaining and well-designed special activities and guided tours for children.

Palazzo Vecchio, Piazza della Signoria 1. Tel: (055) 276 8224; www.museoragazzi.it. Advance booking necessary.

For current activities, see the 'Città e Ragazzi' pages of *Firenze Spettacolo*; *www.firenzespettacolo.it*

Pinocchio Theme Park

A favourite attraction, the **Parco di Pinocchio** at Collodi lies about 15km (9 miles) east of Lucca. The Pinocchio of this theme park is not to be confused with the bland confection served up by Walt Disney. The book *The Adventures of Pinocchio* has, for Italians, the same significance as *Alice in Wonderland* has for the British, or *Huckleberry Finn* for Americans.

Pinocchio's creator, Carlo Lorenzini (1826–90), was born in Florence but he spent much of his childhood in Collodi where his uncle was the custodian of the splendid Villa Garzoni (*see p133*). Fond memories of his childhood led Lorenzini to adopt

Collodi as his pen name, and Collodi the town returned the favour by creating this theme park in the 1950s. The park is located right in the centre of town. Allow at least half a day to enjoy its attractions; there is also an excellent restaurant and good picnic facilities.
Tel: (0572) 429 342/613; www.pinocchio.it. Open: daily 8am–sunset.

Pistoia Zoo
Giardino Zoologico
Via Pieve a Celle 160, Pistoia. Tel: (0573) 911 219; www.zoodipistoia.it. Open: Mon–Fri 9am–6.30pm, Sat & Sun 9am–7pm. Admission charge.

Pinocchio is ingrained into Italian culture – here, a friendly Pinocchio doll welcomes visitors to a Tuscan restaurant

Sport and leisure

It is a debatable point whether sport or music comes first in the affections of many Italians. In Florence, love of sport led the city to commission the great architect Pier Luigi Nervi (who built the Audience Hall in the Vatican) to create the Stadio Comunale in 1932 – a remarkable modern building used to host part of the 1990 Football World Cup. Quite apart from spectator sport, Tuscany's mountains, rivers, bridlepaths and coastline offer plenty of opportunity for active participation in a number of sports.

Cycling

Walk into any bar in Tuscany on a Sunday afternoon, and chances are that if the television is not tuned into a football match, then it will be covering a cycle race. The northern Italians love this gruelling sport and a lot of sponsorship money is poured into supporting top cyclists. If you want more information, the best place to look is on the sports pages of the local papers, but you can also contact the following branches of the organisation that controls the sport, the **Federazione Ciclistica Italiana** (*Via Lugno Il Mugnone 48. Tel: (055) 552 2660; www.federiciclismo.it*).
Florence by Bike offers bike rentals and cycling tours of Florence and the surrounding countryside (*Via San Zanobi 91/R-120-122/R, Firenze, tel: (055) 488 992; www.florencebybike.it*).

Fishing

Tuscany's rivers – in their upper reaches at least – are clean and offer lively sport to anglers. There are also scores of small lakes and rivers that are deliberately stocked with fish – some so tame that they will eat out of your hand. To fish anywhere in the region you need an annual permit. This is very cheap and can be obtained from offices of the **Federazione Italiana della Pesca Sportiva**. There are branches of this organisation in every provincial capital in Tuscany (just ask at the local tourist office), or you can go to the office in Florence (*Via Gordigiani 14, 50122 Firenze, tel: (055) 354 907; www.fipsas.it*). As well as issuing permits, the organisation will provide you with advice and information on fishing times and places.

Football

If you are wandering around the Campo dei Miracoli in Pisa on a Sunday afternoon during the football season, your thoughts on the aesthetic beauty of the Leaning Tower and the cathedral are likely to be rudely interrupted by the roaring, singing and chanting of football supporters watching a game in the massive stadium that stands just to the north of the city walls. Football is as popular in Tuscany today as gladiatorial combats were in ancient Rome. It used to be that the crowds were far more good-natured, but recently violence has marred the sport as in some other parts of Europe. In Florence it's better not to flaunt the opposing team's colours on match day. While Tuscany's top team is the Florentine side, Fiorentina, other teams to watch include Siena, Empoli and Livorno, also first-division (Serie A) teams. Tickets for the Fiorentina can be purchased in bars adjacent to the Stadio Comunale Artemio Franchi, part of the huge sports complex on the Campo di Marte on the eastern edge of the city, including **Bar Marisa** (*Via Carnesecchi 1*) and **Bar Stadio** (*Viale Manfredo Fanti 3r*).

Golf

Acquabona
Portoferraio, Elba. Tel: (0565) 940 066; www.elbagolfacquabona.com

Casentino
Poppi. Tel: (0575) 529 810; www.casentinogolfarezzo.net

Cosmopolitan
Tirrenia. Tel: (050) 33633; www.cosmopolitangolf.it

Florence Ugolino
Grassina. Tel: (055) 205 1009; www.golfugolino.it

Fontevivo
San Miniato. Tel: (0571) 419 012; www.fontevivogolf.it

Hermitage
Portoferraio, Elba. Tel: (0565) 9740.

Le Pavoniere
Prato. Tel: (0574) 620 855; www.golfclubpavoniere.com

Montecatini 'La Pievaccia'
Monsummano. Tel: (0572) 62218.

Poggio dei Medici
Scarperia. Tel: (055) 843 0436; www.poggiodeimedici.com

Explore a scenic road in Tuscany

Punta Ala
Punta Ala. Tel: (0564) 922 121;
www.puntaala.net/golf
Tirrenia
Tirrenia. Tel: (050) 37518;
www.golftirrenia.it
Versilia
Pietrasanta. Tel: (0584) 881 574;
www.versiliagolf.com

Horse riding

Riding and trekking are both very popular pastimes in Tuscany (and even more so in neighbouring Umbria) so, not surprisingly, there is no shortage of opportunities to take a riding holiday. Quite a number of rural hotels offer riding as an option and will make all the necessary arrangements for you. Alternatively, you can contact **FITETREC**, the Federazione Italiana Turismo Equestre e TREC (*tel: (06) 326 50231; www.fitetrec-ante.it/toscana*) for further information, or just pay a visit to any of the following riding clubs:

FLORENCE
Badia Montescalari
Via Montescalari 129, La Panca.
Tel: (050) 959 596.
Centro Ippico Toscano
Via Vespucci 5. Tel: (055) 315 621;
www.centroippicotoscano.it

PISA
Alfea Mensa Artieri
Viale delle Cascine 149. Tel: (050) 53381.
Associazione Ippica Pisana
Via dei Porcari 2, Tirrenia.

Tel: (050) 561 451.
Centro Equitazione e Turismo Equestre
Via Roma, località La Certosa, Calci.
Tel: (050) 938 447.

SIENA
Club Ippico Senese
Strada di Pian del Lago, Monteriggiori.
Tel: (0577) 318 316;
www.clubippicosenese.it
Communita Montana della Garfagnana Offers a more ambitious programme: a waymarked horse-riding trail through the mountains of the Garfagnana region, stopping overnight at 16 staging posts, each of which provides lodgings, a restaurant and stabling.
Castelnuovo di Garfagnana.
Tel: (0583) 641 308; www.cm-garfagnana.lu.it

Horse racing
FLORENCE
For information on race meetings in Cascine Park, contact:
Ippodromo Visarno–Le Cascine
Via del Pegaso 1. Tel: (055) 422 6076.

PISA
Ippodromo di San Rossore
Parco di San Rossore. Tel: (050) 52611;
www.sanrossore.it

Hunting
This is a highly emotive subject in Italy. The opening of the hunting season in September is signalled by a deafening

fusillade of shots spoiling the peace of the Tuscan countryside.

Locals complain bitterly about town dwellers, dressed as if for guerrilla warfare and with an alarmingly casual attitude towards their lethal weapons, virtually laying siege to isolated farmhouses and hamlets whose terrified inhabitants dare not walk in their own fields for fear of stray shots.

Since the start of the hunting season coincides with the grape harvest, when scores of people are spread out among, and partially concealed by, the grape vines, there is further ground for accidents and for conflict between locals and incoming hunters.

The Italian government is also uneasily aware of Italy's bad international reputation for blasting migratory songbirds out of the sky. Increasing restrictions on hunting are being applied, but frequently ignored.

Having said that, there are rigorous restrictions concerning the import of firearms into the country. The **Federazione Italiana della Caccia** (Hunting Federation: at *Via Crispi 49, Pisa, tel: (050) 20331; www.federcaccia.org*) is a useful contact.

Rowing

For rowing on the Arno in Florence, contact the **Canottieri Firenze Comunali** (*Lungarno Ferrucci 2, tel: (055) 681 2151; www.canottiericomunalifirenze.it*). The more up-market **Società Canottieri Firenze** (*www.canottierifirenze.it*) has a delightful clubhouse and landing stage near the Ponte Vecchio at Lungarno de'AML Medici 8 (*tel: (055) 282 130*). In Pisa contact **La Federazione Italiana Nuoto**, Canoa e Canottaggio, Via Mazzini 138 (*tel: (050) 500 870; www.federnuoto.it*).

Scuba diving and underwater fishing

Special permits are issued by the provincial Harbour Master's office. Only over-16s may use underwater guns and similar equipment. When submerged, an underwater fisherman

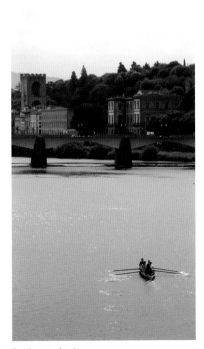

Rowing on the Arno

must indicate the fact with a float bearing a red flag with a yellow diagonal stripe, and must operate within a radius of 50m (55yds) of the support barge or the float bearing the flag. Fishing is prohibited within 50m (55yds) of a beach used by bathers, from fishing installations, or ships at anchor.

For further information, contact:

Centro Sub Pisa
Via dei Condotti 52, Asciano.
Tel: (334) 978 9126;
www.centrosubpisa.com

Sports and fitness centres
FLORENCE
Palestra Porta Romana
Via G Silvani 5. Tel: (055) 232 1799.
Palestra Ricciardi
Borgo Pinti 75. Tel: (055) 247 8444;
www.palestraricciardi.it
Silhouette Club
Viale dei Mille 97.
Tel: (055) 571 488.
Tropos
Via Orcagna 20/a. Tel: (055) 678 381;
www.troposclub.it
Vivarium
Via Accursio 4/r. Tel: (055) 204 7471;
www.vivariumcenter.com
Yoga
Via Bardi 5. Tel: (055) 234 2703.

PISA
Alhambra
Via Fermi 27. Tel: (050) 29111.
Green Park Wellness
Via dei Tulipani, Calambrone. Tel: (050) 313 5711; www.greenparkresort.com

Mithos Centro Wellness
Via S Marco 15. Tel: (050) 47050;
www.mithoscentrowellness.com
Scuola Yoga Sadhana
Via Giunta Pisano 16. Tel: (050) 560 557; www.comune.pisa.it/sadhana
World Fitness Club
Via Garibaldi 69. Tel: (050) 544 360.

SIENA
Gold Gym
Via Fiera Vecchia 9.
Tel: (0577) 285 272; www.goldgym.it
Mens Sana
Viale A Sclavo. Tel: (0577) 47298;
www.mensana.it
Palestra Accademia
Via Mencatelli 5–7.
Tel: (0577) 281 081;
www.accademiasiena.it
The Best Body
Via Leonardo da Vinci 17, Sinalunga.
Tel: (0577) 678 695; www.thebestbody.it

Swimming
Almost the entire Tuscan coastline has sea-bathing facilities, of varying quality. The most developed area is between Marina di Pisa and Marina di Carrara (*see pp126–7*). Most towns have at least one open-air swimming pool (*piscina*).

FLORENCE
These pools are open June to September.
Piscina Bellariva
Lungarno A Moro. Tel: (055) 677 521.
Piscina Costoli
Viale Paoli. Tel: (055) 623 6027.

Piscina le Pavoniere
The most popular.
Cascine Park. Tel: (055) 367 506.

PISA
Piscina Comunale
Via A Pisano. Tel: (050) 531 448.

SIENA
Piscina Acquacalda
Via Bianchi. Tel: (0577) 52667.
Piscina Comunale
Piazza G Amendola. Tel: (0577) 44605.

Tennis
FLORENCE
Circolo Tennis alle Cascine
Tel: (055) 354 326.

PISA
Tennis Club Pisa
Piazzale dello Sport. Tel: (050) 530 313;
www.tennisclubpisa.it

SIENA
Circolo Tennis La Racchetta
Via Vivaldi 2. Tel: (0577) 221 110.

Trekking
Several firms specialise in walking holidays, including **Amiata Trekking & Biking** (*Via Mario Sbrilli 17, Abbadia San Salvatore, Siena, tel: (333) 940 2001; www.trekkingbike.it*), founded in 1989 by trekking enthusiasts. Amiata organises sporting holidays in Tuscany, including skiing, mountain-biking and canoeing, to suit your level of skill. For independent travellers, the *Annuario*

delle Strutture Ricettive della Toscana is an invaluable guide with suggested itineraries and maps.

In addition, the oldest national hiking organisation in Italy, the **Club Alpino Italiano** (*www.cai.it*), offers in-depth information on trail systems all over Italy.

Local branches in Tuscany can suggest maps and information on trekking in the area. Check with: **C.A.I. Firenze** (*Via del Mezzetta 2m, tel: (055) 612 0467*). In Siena, check with **C.A.I. Siena** (*Viale Mazzini 95, tel: (0577) 270 666*).

Winter sports
At Abetone, on the border with Emilia Romagna and 50km (31 miles) north of Pistoia, is Tuscany's main winter sports resort and one of the best Italian ski resorts; it is favoured by wealthy visitors, and has good hotels and restaurants, numerous ski-lifts and splendid mountain scenery. It is just as popular in summer, when many hotels do inexpensive packages. The *Settimane Bianche* (White Week) packages include the cost of a room, all meals and ski passes. The *Settimane Verdi* (Green Week) packages offer accommodation, meals, trekking, tennis and swimming. Packages are easily booked through travel agents.

For more information on winter sports, contact:
Federazione Italiana Sport Invernali (*Viale dei Mille 90, 50121 Firenze, tel: (055) 576 987; www.fisi.org*).

Food and drink

For Italians, food is part of an important social and aesthetic experience – that is one of the reasons why everything closes down for the lunch hour, which actually lasts for the whole afternoon. Junk food is virtually unknown, except in the larger cities, and fast-food chains such as McDonald's and Wimpy are few and far between. Even in modest little restaurants, meals are served with a certain style and the food is almost invariably excellent.

Prices and charges

Prices are perfectly fair, varying according to the type of establishment. In an average restaurant you can expect to pay €15–20 a head for your meal. In addition you will find *servizio* (service charge – usually 15 per cent) and *pane e coperto* (literally 'bread and tablecloth') of up to €1–2 per person; for this you should get a basket full of fresh bread. You could be charged again if you order extra bread, although this may become illegal.

Many restaurants serve *prezzo fisso* (fixed price) meals, costing from around €10–15. This usually consists of a choice of first course (soup or pasta), a choice of main-course dishes (often plainly roasted pork, lamb or chicken) served with a vegetable or salad, plus fruit or cheese. Some restaurants also include a bottle of mineral water or a 25cl (½pt) carafe of table wine and the price includes both service and cover charges; this is referred to as *menù turistico*. In upmarket restaurants the customer is expected to order a full three- (or even four-) course meal. In humbler establishments it is acceptable to order just one dish (say, a plate of pasta).

Picnic food

If you want to eat cheaply, especially at lunchtime, a pleasant alternative to eating in a restaurant is to create a picnic from the delicacies sold at an *alimentari* (grocer's shop). Grocers sell an incredible range of pickled, preserved and cured foods. Apart from the ubiquitous salami, you could sample artichoke hearts (*carciofi*), smoked boar (*cinghiale*), roast quail (*quaglia*), anchovies (*acciughe*) and many other savoury treats. The measure for this kind of food is the *etto* (*uno etto* – one *etto* – is 100g/3½oz), sufficient for two or three people. With bread, fruit, cheese and a bottle of wine you could build up an excellent picnic for two for around €10. Do remember to do your shopping before 1pm, however, as most *alimentari* close at this time and do not open again until 3.30pm or later.

Cheap eats

Another inexpensive alternative, found in most towns of any size, is the *tavola calda* (literally 'hot table'), a self-service restaurant where the cover and service charges are included in the clearly displayed price of each dish. You can either choose a single item, such as a plate of *lasagne*, or you can have a complete meal.

Of course, to many people Italy is synonymous with pizza and, within Tuscany itself, this relatively humble dish is undergoing something of a revival – Florence and Siena both have excellent *pizzerie* specialising in the genuine article, cooked in a wood-fired oven. Various kinds of wood, including chestnut, olive and grape vine, are used to fire the pizza oven, and the gentle smoky fragrance adds something extra to even the plainest of pizzas.

Dine by night in the Piazza della Signoria

Oil and wine

Oil and wine, along with bread, pasta, tomatoes and olives, are among the great staples of the Italian diet. In shops specialising in wine and oil (*vini e olio*) there may well be as wide a range of olive oils on offer as there are wines. Restaurants will boast that their oil comes from their own olive groves: others will offer you a choice, as they would a wine list. Tuscans, in short, treat olive oil seriously.

Oil quality

Olive oil varies greatly in flavour from area to area even though the groves may be only a few kilometres apart. Like vintage wine, the best-quality oils proudly state on the label exactly where they are from. The very finest quality, known as *Extra Vergine*, is that obtained from the first pressing and it has an acidity level of less than one per cent. After the first pressing, the mash is progressively heated to extract the remaining oil, but the quality deteriorates with each subsequent pressing.

Italian wines

Italy is the world's largest producer of wine, although the Italians rank just behind the French in actual consumption. Italian wines are not as popular overseas as French, not because they are inherently inferior but because their marketing has never been as good. This in itself reflects the immense range of wines produced, with every little village making its own local wine. Tuscany led the way in imposing some kind of order when, in 1924, a consortium of Chianti wine growers banded together to produce quality wine to a consistent formula proposed by one of the area's largest vine growers, Barone Bettino Ricasoli. The consortium has since adopted the Gallo Nero (Black Cockerel) as its symbol, and this is now universally recognised as a sign of a very drinkable, soft and fruity wine.

After World War II the Italian government instituted the DOC (Denominazione di Origine Controllata) system whereby the label had to state the place of origin of the wine. In 1966, San Gimignano, near Siena, became the first locality to adopt the DOC system for its delicious and crisp dry white Vernaccia wines. Many growers dislike government control over their wines, and there are certainly many excellent wines that do not have the DOC label, but it does help to give some guidance to the uninitiated.

A sign at a Tuscan vineyard advertises oil and wine for sale

Enoteca Italiana

The best place in all of Italy – not just Tuscany – to get an idea of the range of Italian wines is the Enoteca Italiana in the Medici fortress – Forte di Santa Barbara – in Siena (*see pp117–18*). The venue itself is extremely attractive. You descend by a beautiful curving brick staircase to the main showroom deep within the bastions of this 16th-century fortress. Here, arranged like precious objects in a jeweller's shop, the wines are grouped by their place of origin. Upstairs is a bar and another showroom frequently used for special exhibitions. A free booklet lists the 227 wines available. In the bar you can buy wine to sample either by the glass or by the bottle, at very fair prices for a generous glass. For maximum pleasure, it is highly recommended to take your glass on to the terrace under the great wall of the castle and taste at your leisure, preferably as the sunset turns the sky and the rooftops of Siena a lovely roseate red.

Tel: (0577) 288 811. Open: Apr–Sept Mon noon–8pm, Tue–Sat noon–1am; Oct–Mar Tue–Wed noon–8pm, Thur–Sat noon–1am.

Italian food

The three main meals of the day in Italy are *colazione* or *prima colazione* (breakfast), *pranzo* (lunch) and *cena* (dinner).

Colazione can be, for non-Italians, the least satisfactory of all, since many Italians are content to start their day with a thimbleful of strong black coffee and some kind of cake. If you are unable to face a sugary doughnut first thing in the morning, most bars also have a selection of savouries, such as salami-filled rolls. If you want coffee made with milk ask for *caffè latte*; alternatively you can ask for *cappuccino* (so-called because the frothed-up milk poured on top of the coffee is the same colour as the cowl of a Capuchin monk).

Pranzo (lunch) is often the main meal of the day on Sunday and is served around 1pm. During the rest of the week, *cena* (dinner, served from 8pm) is the main meal. Restaurants serve pretty much the same menu at lunch and in the evening. A full meal can consist of up to four courses with a bewildering range of choice, especially at the *antipasto* stage; the mouth-watering range of appetisers on offer may include salami in half a dozen forms, seafood served hot or cold, and all kinds of pickled or preserved vegetables (in some restaurants, *antipasti* are frequently displayed on a table for you to serve yourself).

Next comes the *primo piatto* (first course); this consists of pasta, rice or soup in any one of 100 different varieties. The *secondo piatto* (main course) consists of meat or fish accompanied by a *contorno* (side dish) of vegetables or salad (side dishes are priced separately and are entirely optional). Last of all, you can choose between fruit (*frutta*), cheese (*formaggio*) or a dessert (*dolce*).

If you want to try the local wine, you can ask for a quarter, half or litre carafe. *Vino da tavola* (table wine) is both good and cheap. Branded wine, even from the locality, is likely to be much more expensive.

Italy used to have two main types of restaurant, the *trattoria* and the *ristorante*. Originally, the *trattoria* was a humbler family-run establishment. With increasing professionalisation of the catering trade, the *trattoria* has become increasingly hard to find – where they do exist, they still tend to be cheaper than the *ristorante*. An old name being revived is the *osteria* (hostelry). This can be confusing for visitors and natives alike; sometimes an *osteria* serves rustic and inexpensive food, while, at the other extreme, it can be a trendy, and quite expensive, restaurant.

Tuscan specialities

Tuscan food is, essentially, country food – hearty, chunky and highly flavoured. An example of how it combines frugality with flavour is *bruschetta*, bread rubbed with garlic and brushed with olive oil, then toasted. Beans figure

A traditional Florentine *enoteca*

Lucca you get a superb *minestra di farro*, soup to which grains of wheat are added. Arezzo offers *pappardelle alla lepre*, long flat pasta flavoured with hare sauce. Siena is renowned for *panforte*, a rich cake made of honey, nuts and fruit, originally made to sustain pilgrims on their journeys.

If you like good food, the best approach is to experiment: waiters are proud of their work and will do their best to describe the ingredients of any unfamiliar dish – which may well be unknown to Italians from other parts of the country as well as to you.

Where to eat

The following star ratings are based on the cost of a full meal per person, excluding drinks:

★	up to €12
★★	€12–22
★★★	more than €22

FLORENCE

Il Bargello ★★

Standard, economical fare; near the Bargello Museum.
Piazza Signoria 4r. Tel: (055) 214 071; www.ilbargello.net. Closed: Mon.

Cantina Barbagianni ★★

Stylish cellar-bar restaurant.
Via Sant'Egidio 13r.
Tel: (055) 248 0508;
www.cantinabarbagianni.it.
Closed: Sat lunch & Sun.

La Casalinga ★★

Family-run, economical and popular restaurant.

in a variety of forms, and other Italians refer to Tuscans as *mangiafagioli* – the bean-eaters. *Fagiolini* consist of green beans, usually served cold with olive oil. *Fagioli* are white beans served with a variety of dressings. *Zuppa di fagioli* is bean soup. *Ribollita* (meaning 'reboiled') is solid soup cooked to the point that all the stock is absorbed into the bread and vegetables. *Zuppa di verdura* is a thick soup of green vegetables, such as cabbage.

Apart from these staples, almost every city has its own speciality. In Pisa you can get *ciechi alla pisana*, baby eels cooked in garlic and tomatoes (and of course a wide range of other fish dishes). Florence offers *bistecca alla fiorentina*, a massive steak brushed with olive oil and grilled over charcoal, and *trippa alla fiorentina*, strips of tripe braised in tomato sauce and garlic. In

Via dei Michelozzi 9r. Tel: (055) 218 624. Closed: Sun & 3 weeks Aug.

Enoteca Pinchiorri ★★★
One of Italy's best restaurants, renowned for its amazing wine list and garden courtyard.
Via Ghibellina 87. Tel: (055) 242 777; www. enotecapinchiorri.com. Closed: all day Sun & Mon.

Le Fonticine ★★
Traditional, sophisticated, cosy restaurant, mindful of the tourist trade.
Via Nazionale 79r. Tel: (055) 282 106; www.lefonticine.com. Closed: Sun & Mon & month of Aug.

Golden View Open Bar ★★
Restaurant, wine bar and jazz club with huge windows overlooking the Ponte Vecchio.
Via dei Bardi 58r. Tel: (055) 214 502; www. goldenviewopenbar.com

La Grotta Guelfa ★
Tucked away on a loggia just behind the Mercato Nuovo, this is one of the few places in the city centre where you can eat cheaply in the open. Very

popular with locals.
Via Pellicceria 5r. Tel: (055) 210 042.

Harry's Bar ★★★
This is a clone of the more famous bar in Venice, serving American-style cocktails and burgers.
Lungarno A Vespucci 22r. Tel: (055) 239 6700; www.harrysbarfirenze.it. Closed: Sun.

Hotel Westin Excelsior ★★★
Two choices here, both sumptuous: the Edwardian opulence of the ground-floor bar, or the roof-terrace restaurant with its superb views.
Piazza Ognissanti 3. Tel: (050) 264 201.

La Loggia ★★★
Restaurant with a view, high on the hill to the south of the city.
Piazzale Michelangelo 1. Tel: (055) 234 2832.

Il Mandarino ★★
Chinese restaurant close to the Ponte Vecchio.
Via Condotta 17r. Tel: (055) 239 6130. Closed: Mon.

Onice ★★★
Chic Michelin-starred restaurant with panoramic views of the city.

Villa La Vedetta, Viale Michelangelo 78. Tel: (055) 681 631; www. villalavedettahotel.com

Osteria del Cinghiale Bianco ★★★
Friendly and busy family *trattoria* south of the river; advisable to book.
Borgo San Jacopo 43r. Tel: (055) 215 706; www.cinghialebianco.it. Closed: Wed lunch.

Il Pizzaiuolo ★★
Renowned for its top-class Neapolitan pizzas in a buzzing rustic environment.
Via de'Macci 113r. Tel: (055) 241 171. Closed: Sun.

Trattoria Angiolino ★★★
Traditional Florentine *trattoria* in the narrow streets of the Oltrarno district, known to locals and knowing visitors.
Via Santo Spirito 36r. Tel: (055) 239 8976.

Trattoria Palle d'Oro ★★
Busy marketplace *trattoria* at lunchtime, cosy rustic atmosphere in the evening.
Via Sant'Antonino 43–45r. Tel: (055) 288 383. Closed: Sun & Aug.

Trattoria Quattro Leoni ★★

Set in a small, intimate square in the Oltrarno district, this is a popular meeting place for artists.
Via dei Vellutini 1r.
Tel: (055) 218 562;
www.4leoni.com

Il Vegetariano ★★

Excellent vegetarian restaurant with a large array of desserts.
Via delle Ruote 30r.
Tel: (055) 475 030.
Closed: Sat, Sun, Mon lunch.

AREZZO

La Buca di San Francesco ★★

Consciously arty but it has good local food.
Via San Francesco 1.
Tel: (0575) 23271; www. bucadisanfrancesco.it.
Closed: Mon evening & Tue; 2 weeks in July.

Il Cantuccio ★★

Typical Aretino dishes are prepared in this homely cellar restaurant.
Via Madonna del Prato 76. Tel: (0575) 26830;
www.il-cantuccio.it

Logge Vasari ★★★

An ideal place for a leisurely lunch; while you dine, you can sit and look out on to the Piazza Grande from the shade of Vasari's loggia.
Piazza Grande.
Tel: (0575) 300 333;
www.starsweb.it/sito/ loggevasari.
Closed: Tue.

CASTELLINA IN CHIANTI

Tenuta di Ricavo ★★★

Elegant, traditional Tuscan restaurant. Located in a little hamlet 3km (2 miles) north of Castellina.
Tel: (0577) 740 221;
www.ricavo.com.
Closed: Sun.

GREVE IN CHIANTI

Bottega del Moro ★★★

Excellent, friendly restaurant specialising in regional dishes such as *zuppa di funghi* (soup made from a variety of wild mushrooms).
Piazza Trieste 14r.
Tel: (055) 853 753.
Closed: Mon.

LUCCA

Il Buca di Sant' Antonio ★★★

Rustic-style upmarket restaurant specialising in local cuisine. Booking advisable.
Via della Cervia 1–3.
Tel: (0583) 55881;

The small and stylish Il Bargello

www.bucadisantantonio. com. Closed: Sun eve & Mon, last 3 weeks of Jan & last 3 weeks of Aug.

Caffeteria San Colombano ★★

This trendy urban dining room and bar is set inside the ramparts of the city wall.

Baluardo San Colombano 10. Tel: (0583) 464 641; www.caffeteriasancolomba no.it. Closed: Mon.

Rusticanella 2 ★

Cheap, cheerful and

excellent for a quick lunch.

Via San Paolino 32. Tel: (0583) 55383. Closed: Sun.

MONTECATINI TERME

Cucco ★★★

This restaurant combines good atmosphere and service with high-quality and innovative cuisine.

Via del Salsero 3. Tel: (0572) 72765. Closed: Tue & Wed lunch.

MONTEFIORALLE

Taverna del Guerrino ★★

Set in part of the city walls and with stunning views, this family-run *taverna* serves up Tuscan specialities.

Tel: (055) 85 31 06. Closed: Mon all year & Tue & Wed in winter.

PISA

Antica Trattoria 'Da Bruno' ★

Recommended and lively old *trattoria* serving fresh seasonal produce.

Via Luigi Bianchi 12. Tel: (050) 560 818. Closed: Mon pm & Tue.

L'Artilafo Club ★★★

The six small dining rooms lend a cosy feel to this lively restaurant.

Via San Martino 33. Tel: (050) 27010; www.lartilafo.it. Closed: Sun.

Osteria dei Cavalieri ★★★

The well-prepared food in this *osteria* includes home-made pasta and a good selection of vegetarian dishes.

Via San Frediano 16. Tel: (050) 580 858; www. osteriacavalieri.pisa.it. Closed: Sat lunch & Sun.

Dining is a sociable event in the open-air cafés of Siena

Osteria del Violino ★★
Medium-size restaurant serving regional cuisine; wine cellar attached.
Via la Tinta 25.
Tel: (050) 49851;
www.osteriadelviolino.it.
Closed: Tue.

Osteria La Toscana ★★
Seasonal Tuscan dishes with a vegetarian option on the menu.
Piazzetta Tongiorgi 1/3.
Tel: (050) 554 557.
Closed: Mon in winter.

Pizzeria Bella Napoli ★
This restaurant/pizzeria offers a very economical lunchtime tourist menu during the week.
Via del Borghetto 44.
Tel: (050) 578 520;
www.bellanapoli-pisa.it.
Closed: Mon.

Al Re Artù ★
Tuscan cuisine and a garden.
Via Santa Maria 129.
Tel: (050) 831 2130.

Al Ristoro dei Vecchi Macelli ★★★
Despite its somewhat off-putting name (The Old Slaughterhouses), this is one of Pisa's most upmarket restaurants.
Via Volturno 49. Tel:
(050) 20424. Closed: Wed
& Sun lunchtime.

La Tana ★
Friendly, rambling and boisterous *tavola calda.*
Via San Frediano 6.
Tel: (050) 580 540.
Closed: Sat lunch & Sun.

Taverna di Pillo ★★
Popular with students, this restaurant offers organic dishes prepared in the Tuscan tradition.
Via del Borghetto 39.
Tel: (050) 571 467.
Closed: Wed.

SAN GIMIGNANO
Enoteca il Castello ★★
This *enoteca* (wine bar), within a medieval *palazzo*, is outstanding for its service, wines, Tuscan specialities including *cinghiale* (wild boar), ambience and views.
Via del Castello 20.
Tel: (0577) 940 878;
www.enotecacastello.it

SIENA
Guidoriccio ★★
Rustic cellar restaurant near the Campo.
Via Dupré 2. Tel: (0577)
44350. Closed: Sun.

Mugolone ★★★
Well-prepared meat dishes and traditional recipes.
Via dei Pellegrini 8.

Tel: (0577) 283 235.
Closed: Thur & Sun pm.

L'Osteria (dei Rossi) ★★
Head here for a great-value simple Tuscan menu.
Via dei Rossi 79. Tel:
(0577) 287 592.

Osteria 'l Grattacielo' ★
Tiny cabin on the corner of Via dei Pontani and Via dei Termi. Communal tables, no menu and only cold food – but queues testify to the value.
Via Pontani 8.
Tel: (0577) 289 326.
Closed: Sun, part of
June & Nov.

Osteria Le Logge ★★★
Traditional *trattoria* serving gourmet dishes at good prices.
Via del Porrione 33. Tel:
(0577) 48013. Closed: Sun.

Ristorante Da Renzo ★★
Pleasant, family-run restaurant with excellent table wine and a good fixed-price menu.
Via delle Terme 14.
Tel: (0577) 289 296.
Closed: Thur.

Trombicche ★
Busy. Daily change in menu; local specialities.
Via della Terme 66.
Tel: (0577) 288 089.
Closed: Sun.

La vendemmia (the harvest)

Two great harvests take place every year in Tuscany, one of grapes and the other of olives. Grape vines and olive trees grow companionably side by side, flourishing in the same conditions of soil and sun. Their harvesting, however, takes place at different seasons.

The grape harvest begins in the second half of September, and for about a month the villages and small towns are filled with the heady scent of the fermenting fruit. As recently as the 1990s it was possible to see oxen pulling immense wooden containers piled with grapes. Today, they have been superseded by noisy little tractors and trailers. The picking of the grapes, however, is still largely done by hand. This back-breaking and time-consuming process provides employment for casual labourers, including many students and young people from other parts of Europe or from as far afield as the USA and Australia. It is still possible to obtain such work, though wine growers are increasingly turning to mechanisation.

Not all of the grapes are pressed at once. A Tuscan speciality is Vin Santo (literally 'Holy Wine' – so-called because priests are said to love it), made from grapes that are dried in the sun for about ten days after picking. They then become more like raisins and the wine made from them is usually served as a dessert wine accompanied by sweet almond biscuits.

Olive trees live to an immense age, and olive groves are handed down from one generation to another. The trees have to be pruned and manured

Grapes are collected by the bucketful

Tractors are used to gather grapes

every year to ensure that they will bear an abundance of fruit. The olives are usually left on the tree until they turn black and are harvested in December. They too are plucked by hand, the method being to shake or rake the fruit from the tree, catching them in a net suspended beneath. Most of the crop is taken to a mill where they are processed commercially. Some villa estates still process their own crop and sell the product, specially packaged, at a premium price, though these days the pressing is done by machine and the traditional stone wheel, operated by a donkey or horse, is very much a thing of the past.

Hotels and accommodation

Italian hotels are graded on a star system, the best hotels being awarded five stars and those with fewest facilities being awarded one. In general, a five-star hotel really does mean that you will receive five-star treatment – and a five-star bill. Most visitors, however, find three-star hotels perfectly adequate for their needs, offering a comfortable room with bathroom en suite.

The grading system is not always a totally reliable guide to room quality – even four- or three-star hotels have some rooms that are small, dark and cramped – and one- or two-star hotels may have one or two pricey rooms. So, as a rule, it is better to take a look at the bedroom before committing yourself. By law, foreigners are still required to register with the police on arrival in any Italian town, but in practice the hotel will do this automatically, taking your passport when you arrive to fill in the necessary form. There is also a tourist tax, but this will be included in the price of your room, which should be clearly displayed in the room itself.

Breakfast is rarely included in the room price – in any case, hotel breakfasts, except in the most expensive hotels, are rarely worth eating; you would do better to follow the habit of locals and take coffee in a local bar.

Agriturismo (farm holidays)

The changing pattern of rural economics means that more and more farmers are providing tourist accommodation to boost their incomes, sometimes in their homes and sometimes in converted barns and outbuildings.

The whole idea of *agriturismo* is that you should experience farm life (and you often eat with the host family), so you need to speak reasonably good Italian to make the most of it, although some farms offer self-catering accommodation. Details of *agriturismo* holidays are to be found in the *Annual Register of Tuscan Accommodation* (*see opposite*).

There are three agencies in Florence: **Consorzio Terre di Firenze** (*Piazza San Firenze 3, tel: (055) 599 600; www.terredifirenze.it*); **Turismo Verde Toscana** (*Via Iacopo Nardi 41, tel: (055) 233 8911; www.turismoverde.it*); and **Terranostra Toscana** (*Via della Villa Demidoff 64/D, tel: (055) 324 5655; www.terranostra.it*).

Alberghi per la gioventù (youth hostels)

There are 12 youth hostels in Tuscany, but some of them are only open during the summer – Easter to the end of September. The facilities are usually basic. There is no age limit for the use of these hostels (in fact, senior citizens get discounts!), and you can join on the spot by buying a guest card from any hostel. With the exception of the Santa Monica hostel in Florence, all provide meals. Usually closed: 9am–3.30pm.

For further details, contact the head office for a map and list of hostel addresses: **Associazione Italiana Alberghi per la Gioventù** (AIG), *Via Cavour 44, 00184 Roma (tel: (06) 487 1152; www.ostellionline.org).*

Rustic style in San Gimignano

Albergo diurno (day hotel)

This highly civilised facility, which you would like more countries to adopt, seems to be on the way out even in the country of its origin. The day hotel is a boon of incalculable value to a traveller passing through a city. Open 6am–midnight, the *albergo diurno* provides all that you expect to find in an ordinary hotel, except overnight accommodation. For instance, the baths at the *albergo diurno* at Montecatini Terme railway station are even supplied with water from the spa. Usually, day hotels are located in, or very close to, the main railway station.

Annuario delle Strutture e Ricettive della Toscana (Annual Register of Tuscan Accommodation)

This comprehensive annual publication is an invaluable reference work, written in Italian, French, German, Spanish and English. It is far more than just a simple listing of hotels: it also covers holiday villages, camping sites, farmhouse accommodation and trekking centres. The publication is divided into Tuscany's 13 official tourist districts, and each section includes a useful map of the area.

Running to over 700 pages, the *Annuario* is not the kind of handbook the average traveller will want to carry around, but it is very useful for advance planning. Every hotel will have its own copy, so if you want to look something up just ask at the reception.

Hotel chain

An Italian hotel chain worth knowing about is **Family Hotels and Restaurants** (*Viale Don Minzoni 11r, Firenze, tel: (055) 333 403; www.familyhotels.com*), an association of independent hotels which all have in common the fact that they are family-run. Many are in 17th- to 18th-century buildings and are graded three-star.

Locande

The *locanda* is the cheapest form of accommodation, apart from youth hostels. In a village or small town, a *locanda* could consist of a couple of rooms above a restaurant. In a large city it is more frequently a room in a family home. Using a *locanda* brings you into direct contact with the locals, so you need some knowledge of spoken Italian.

Local tourist offices will give you details of *locande* (plural of *locanda*) in their area.

Monasteries and pilgrim hostels

The monastic tradition is still strong in Italy, and you do not have to be religiously inclined to take advantage of monastic hospitality – all you have to do is pay a very modest sum for lodgings. If there is no fixed charge you should make a donation equivalent to the rate for a one-star hotel. Check with the local tourist boards or the archdiocese of the nearest city what is available in the area.

NOISE

The only way to escape Florence's cacophony – car horns, wailing sirens, motor scooters, domestic discord, buses, early-morning street cleaners and late-night bars – is to stay in a sound-proofed hotel, or flee the city altogether. Avoiding main streets and piazzas, or asking for rooms away from the front of the hotel, cuts down on the racket. Better still, invest in earplugs.

For women travellers, the **Associazione Cattolica al Servizio della Giovane,** or Protezione della Giovane (*www.acisjf.it*), with offices in most major towns and often at major railway stations, can organise accommodation in hostels.

In Siena the **Casa del Pellegrino** in the Santuario di Santa Caterina offers delightful accommodation with views across the city. Although run by nuns, it has accommodation for both sexes; ring the bell by the gate in Via Camporegio (*tel: (0577) 44177*). The only restriction is that you must be in by 11pm, and you cannot get out before 8am without prior arrangement.

Book via *www.ostellionline.org*

Villaggi turistici (tourist villages)

These are groups of custom-built bungalows and apartments, usually located near a popular resort. The bungalows vary in size but usually accommodate four people. Restaurant facilities are available on the site. The *Annual Register of Tuscan Accommodation* contains full details (*see p171*).

Villas

The tremendous wave of building in the 16th and 17th centuries, when every family of substance expected to own a country retreat, has left a legacy of fine rural buildings all over Tuscany, many of which are now let as self-catering accommodation, complete with swimming pool and gardens (some even come complete with servants). The rental costs look high but can work out very reasonably if the party is large enough. Most major travel agents can arrange bookings. Specialist agencies (as well as individual owners) advertise in the classified sections of several leading British newspapers.

View of Tuscany from the Vignamaggio winery and hotel, believed to be the house where the *Mona Lisa* was painted

On business

By 1945, Italy was one of the poorest countries in Europe, having endured the gimcrack Fascist regime of the 1930s, followed by the terrible hammering of World War II. However, some four decades later, the Italian economy was growing faster than those of Britain and France. The Italians emerged from what they proudly called Il Sorpasso *(the 'overtaking') as one of the seven most powerful industrial nations in the world.*

Currently the country is experiencing the problems of corruption, in the business and political sphere, and of recession, but no one who knows Italy's track record can doubt that it will emerge triumphant.

An example of Italy's ability to adapt to changing conditions is its attitude to agriculture, the traditional industry. In 1950 it represented 25 per cent of the economy. Since then it has dropped to less than 5 per cent, with industries using new technologies taking over. Italian industry is composed of a handful of giants who operate on an international scale, then a band of some 3,500 middle-range firms. Beneath this is a multiplicity of small operations, underpinning the whole.

Etiquette

Despite the vigorous adoption of new technologies, doing business in Italy means observing traditional customs. Thus, while personal contact is extremely important, it is regarded as the height of bad manners to mix business and pleasure. Do not attempt to do business over a meal, particularly if you are a guest. Wine is central to Italian social life, but drunkenness is rare and regarded with contempt. It is customary to shake hands all round on meeting, and on departure. Titles should always be used. All university graduates, for instance, expect to be addressed as *Dottore* or *Dottoressa*, lawyers as *Avvocato*, architects as *Architetto*, engineers as *Ingegnere*. It is not necessary to use the surname. The Tuscans are very fashion conscious; you will gain greater credibility by dressing well.

Working hours

Tuscany has decided to break with the working hours of the past (which involved a three-hour lunch break) and work the same hours as the rest of Europe: from 9am to 5.30pm. The rest of Italy has yet to follow suit, but more and more businesses are beginning to see the benefits. Where new working hours have yet to be established, office hours run from 8.30am to about 5.30pm. Government offices are only open to the public in the morning. The custom of opening on Saturday morning is rapidly disappearing in favour of the *sabato inglese* ('the English Saturday'). August is the official holiday month all over Italy and it is useless to attempt to make appointments.

Information

The Foreign Department (Commercio Estero) of the **Chamber of Commerce** (Camera di Commercio) in Florence can provide information on local industries: *Piazza dei Giudici 3. Tel: (055) 27951; www.promofirenze.it*

Other Chambers of Commerce are:

Arezzo
Viale Giotto 4.
Tel: (0575) 3030; www.ar.camcom.it
Pisa
Piazza V Emanuele II 5.
Tel: (050) 512 111; www.pi.camcom.it
Prato
Via Valentini 14.
Tel: (0574) 61261; www.po.camcom.it
Siena
Piazza Matteotti 30.
Tel: (0577) 202 511; www.si.camcom.it

Newspapers

Italy's two main daily newspapers, both carrying in-depth business news, are *La Repubblica* (*www.repubblica.it*) and *Corriere della Sera* (*www.corriere.it*). Two other papers are devoted entirely

to financial affairs: the daily newspaper *Il Sole–24 Ore* (*www.ilsole24ore.com*) and the weekly *Italia Oggi* (*www.italiaoggi.it*).

Services

Executive Service
Offers translators, secretaries and office space.
Via Ponte alle Mosse 61, Florence.
Tel: (055) 324 111;
www.executivefirenze.it
International Service
Offers interpreters.
Via della Palancola 20, Florence.
Tel: (055) 575 371; www.inteser.net

Exhibitions and trade fairs

Several historic buildings in Florence have been converted to provide facilities for exhibitions and trade fairs. One of them is the **Palazzo Strozzi** (*see p61*), the venue for one of the biggest and most important antique trade fairs in Italy – the Mostra Mercato Internazionale dell'Antiquariato, held every autumn in odd-numbered years.

Another is the huge **Fortezza da Basso** (*www.firenzefiera.it*) alongside the railway station, built in 1534. Once used as a barracks and prison, it was converted to an exhibition centre in 1967. The interior of the fortress was transformed in 1978 when a new and modernistic exhibition hall was built of steel and aluminium.

Details of the annual programme of trade fairs in Tuscany may be obtained from the tourist office (*see pp188–9*).

Practical guide

Arriving
Passports
To enter Italy, visitors from the EU and Commonwealth countries and the USA need only a valid passport (or identity card for EU nationals). Other nationals may require a visa and should apply for one in advance from an Italian embassy.

By air
Florence Peretola (Amerigo Vespucci) airport is 5km (3 miles) to the northwest of the city. Meridiana operates twice-daily scheduled services to this airport from the UK, Spain, France (Air France), Germany (Lufthansa) and Belgium (SN). Some tour operators offer charter flights in summer. For Peretola information, telephone *(055) 306 1300* or check their website at *www.aeroporto.firenze.it*

Pisa's small, friendly airport, Aeroporto Galileo Galilei, is the main international airport for the region. It is well served by scheduled, budget and charter flights from all over Europe. Opening times of facilities vary, but foreign exchange is available 8am–6pm, except on Sundays. Special toilets and phones are provided for travellers with disabilities. For flight information, telephone *(050) 849 300; www.pisa-airport.com*

It is a short drive from Pisa airport to the two main motorways serving Tuscany, the A12 coastal autostrada and the A11 for Florence and Arezzo. Trains connect the airport station hourly with Pisa (5 minutes) and Florence (1 hour) and with Lucca, Montecatini, Pistoia and Prato.

By rail
The *Thomas Cook European Rail Timetable*, available from Thomas Cook offices in the UK, by phoning *01733 416477*, or buy online at *www.thomascookpublishing.com*, is invaluable for rail users travelling to, and within, Tuscany. Overnight sleeper trains leave daily from Paris Gare de Lyon for Pisa (11½ hours) and Florence (13½ hours). Also see *www.fs-on-line.it*

By road
The most comfortable way to take your car to Italy is by Motorail (summer only). Join at Calais and travel overnight to Livorno (17 hours) or Bologna (16 hours); or from Paris Bercy to Florence (13½ hours) or Bologna (11 hours). Britain is at least 48 hours from Tuscany by road. *www.fs-on-line.it*

Camping
There are more than 200 registered camping sites in Tuscany, with the highest concentration along the coast. The invaluable *Annuario delle Strutture e Ricettive della Toscana* (*see p171*) provides full details. The Italian State Tourist Board (ENIT) also provides

good information on its website:
www.enit.it

Children

Children under four travel free on the
railway; 4–12-year-olds pay half the fare.

Climate

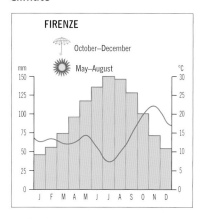

FIRENZE

October–December

May–August

**WEATHER CONVERSION
CHART**

25.4mm = 1 inch

$°F = 1.8 × °C + 32$

April–June and September–October
are the best times to visit Tuscany.
Avoid going there during the very hot
period of July–August, particularly if
you plan to stay in the cities. The
holiday season ends abruptly on
30 September in purely tourist resorts
such as the seaside.

Rain can be expected at any time
during autumn, but is most likely in
September and November. October's
mild, sunny days might be ideal; hotel
prices, too, are reduced after September.

Conversion tables

See p179.

Florence follows the Italian system in
clothing and shoe sizes.

Crime

Pickpockets can be a problem.
If you are robbed you should make
an official report to the police; you
must obtain an official statement in
order to claim insurance.
Multilingual statement forms are
available at the main police station
in Florence (*Via Zara 2, tel: (055)
49771*), and in Pisa (*Via M Lalli,
tel: (050) 583 602;
www.questure.poliziadistato.it* for both
Florence and Pisa).

Customs regulations

The allowances for goods bought
in duty-free shops (in airports or on
board ships and planes), sold free of
customs duty and VAT, apply to anyone
visiting Italy from a country outside
the European Union.

The allowances here are (per
person aged over 17): 200 cigarettes
or 100 cigarillos or 50 cigars or
250g (9oz) of tobacco; 1 litre
(2pts) of spirits or 2 litres (3½pts) of
table wine, and 2 litres (3½pts) of
fortified or sparkling wine; 75cl
(1½pts) of perfume.

Driving

The cities of Tuscany are no place for
the timid driver. Parking is difficult
and traffic excluded from the centre.

But a car is essential if you want to explore rural Tuscany.

Accidents

In the event of an accident, exchange insurance information with the driver(s) of other vehicle(s) involved, inform the police, make a statement and inform your insurance company. Most car-hire companies have a ready-made form with carbon copy to be filled in by both parties in the case of an accident.

Autostrade

Most Italian motorways have tolls. When you join, you will pass through a barrier; stop and press the large red button on the left (driver's side), and you obtain a ticket. Hand this in at the booth when you exit the motorway and a display will tell you what to pay.

Breakdown

Switch the hazard warning lights on immediately and place the red warning triangle 50m (55yds) behind the vehicle on ordinary roads and 100m (109yds) behind the vehicle on motorways (the use of a warning triangle is compulsory outside built-up areas, as is the wearing of a reflector vest for anyone standing outside the car; there is a fine for those who do not comply). Next, find a telephone and ring *116*, the number for the **Automobile Club d'Italia** (ACI), and give the operator your location and the make and registration of the car.

The car will be towed to the nearest ACI-affiliated garage (free of charge to foreign-registered vehicles). It is well worth using this number too if you have an accident: the ACI will help with police formalities and the exchange of insurance details. If necessary they will also help to find a garage for repairs.

There are double telephones every 2km (1 mile) on the *autostrade*: a picture of a wrench for reporting mechanical problems, and of a red cross for calling an ambulance. Road police patrol frequently.

Documents

A valid UK or Republic of Ireland EC-model 'pink' licence is acceptable in Italy. Holders of the older 'green' licence should either exchange it for the new format, or obtain an International Driving Permit (IDP) to accompany the older licence. If you are driving your own car in Italy, carry the registration document and your certificate of insurance. If you are hiring a car in Italy, you need only your licence or IDP.

If you hire a car, collision insurance, often called collision damage waiver or CDW, is normally offered by the hirer, and is usually compulsory. Check with your own motor insurers before you leave, as you may be covered by your normal policy. If not, CDW is payable locally and may be as much as 50 per cent of the hiring fee. Neither CDW nor your personal travel insurance will protect you for liability arising out of an accident in a hired car – for instance, if you damage another vehicle or injure someone. If you are likely to hire a car, you should obtain such extra cover, preferably from your travel agent or other insurer before departure.

Parking

Scarcely any town or city in Tuscany allows cars into the inner city area and there is never enough space in the perimeter car parks to cope with demand in summer. Arrive early to be sure of finding a space. In Florence, the major car parks are all near the main railway station. Where there are blue lines you must pay the attendant. White lines indicate parking for residents only.

Petrol

Petrol prices in Italy are among the highest in Europe. Petrol stations are usually open 7am–12.30pm and 4–7.30pm, Mon–Fri. Many are closed on Sat–Sun, and all close on public holidays, except for *autostrade* service stations. The sign '*Aperto 24 Ore*' means that there is an automatic pump which accepts banknotes. Very few petrol stations accept credit cards. Two types of petrol are sold: *Super* (4-star) and *Super senza piombo* (unleaded). Diesel is sold as *gasolio*.

Rental

Plenty of travel agents offer fly-drive packages to Pisa, where cars can be collected on arrival at the airport. The price should include unlimited mileage

Practical guide

CONVERSION TABLE

FROM	TO	MULTIPLY BY
Inches	Centimetres	2.54
Feet	Metres	0.3048
Yards	Metres	0.9144
Miles	Kilometres	1.6090
Acres	Hectares	0.4047
Gallons	Litres	4.5460
Ounces	Grams	28.35
Pounds	Grams	453.6
Pounds	Kilograms	0.4536
Tons	Tonnes	1.0160

To convert back, for example from centimetres to inches, divide by the number in the third column.

MEN'S SUITS

UK	36	38	40	42	44	46	48
Rest of Europe	46	48	50	52	54	56	58
USA	36	38	40	42	44	46	48

DRESS SIZES

UK	8	10	12	14	16	18
France	36	38	40	42	44	46
Italy	38	40	42	44	46	48
Rest of Europe	34	36	38	40	42	44
USA	6	8	10	12	14	16

MEN'S SHIRTS

UK	14	14.5	15	15.5	16	16.5	17
Rest of Europe	36	37	38	39/40	41	42	43
USA	14	14.5	15	15.5	16	16.5	17

MEN'S SHOES

UK	7	7.5	8.5		9.5	10.5	11
Rest of Europe	41	42	43		44	45	46
USA	8	8.5	9.5		10.5	11.5	12

WOMEN'S SHOES

UK	4.5	5	5.5	6	6.5		7
Rest of Europe	38	38	39	39	40		41
USA	6	6.5	7	7.5	8		8.5

and insurance as well as a 24-hour emergency breakdown service. Hire companies include:

Florence
Avis
Via Borgognissanti 128r. Tel: (055) 213 629; www.avis.com
Europcar
Via Borgognissanti 53r.
Tel: (055) 290 438;
www.europcar.com
Hertz
Via Maso Finiguerra 33r.
Tel: (055) 239 8205/282 260;
www.hertz.com

Florence Airport
Maggiore
Tel: (055) 311 256; www.maggiore.it

Pisa Airport
Avis
Tel: (050) 42028.
Europcar
Tel: (050) 41081.
Maggiore
Tel: (050) 42574.
Hertz
Tel: (050) 43220/49186; and Via Cisanello 168, tel: (050) 950 210.

Siena
Avis
Via Martini 36. Tel: (0577) 270 305.

Rules of the road
Traffic drives on the right. Speed limits are: 50kph (31mph) in built-up areas, 90kph (56mph) on secondary roads, 110kph (68mph) on main roads, and 130kph (81mph) on the *autostrada*. Seat belts must be worn in the front of the car (and in the rear where fitted). Using the horn is prohibited in built-up areas except in emergencies. Outside towns use the horn to warn that you are about to overtake.

Electricity
The supply is 220 volts and most sockets take (round) two-pin plugs. Adaptors are required for most non-Continental appliances and a transformer for 100–120 volt appliances.

Embassies and consulates
Most embassies and consulates are in Rome, but the UK and the USA maintain consulates in Florence.
UK
Lungarno Corsini 2.
Tel: (055) 284 133;
www.britishembassy.gov.uk
USA
Lungarno Amerigo Vespucci 38.
Tel: (055) 266 951;
www.florence.usconsulate.gov

Emergency telephone numbers
Police *tel: 113.*
Fire *tel: 115.*
Ambulance *tel: 118.*

Etiquette
Visitors are expected to be decently dressed, especially when entering churches.

Health

All EU countries have reciprocal arrangements for reclaiming the cost of medical services. UK residents should obtain the European Health Insurance Card (EHIC) from any UK post office or online. Claiming is often a laborious process and you are only covered for medical care, not for emergency repatriation or holiday cancellation. You are therefore advised to take out a travel insurance policy to cover all eventualities. You can purchase such insurance through the AA and most travel agents.

Tuscany presents no unavoidable health hazards. Mosquitoes and other biting insects are the major nuisance, and repellent, as well as ointment to soothe bites, is a good idea.

The summer sun is fierce – adopt a cautious approach to sunbathing.

Postcard stall at Piazzale Michelangelo, Florence

Pharmacists are well qualified to give advice on any minor ailments. If you need emergency help, call **Pronto Soccorso** (First Aid), *tel: 118*.

Lost property

S*ee Crime, p177.* UK and US citizens can contact their consulates in Florence for emergency assistance or advice *(see opposite)*. Florence has a central lost property office: **Ufficio Oggetti Smarriti** (*Via Circondaria 19, tel: (055) 328 3942*).

Maps

Local tourist offices (*see pp188–9*) will provide town maps free of charge.

Media

Tuscany's main newspaper is *La Nazione*. Newspapers from other parts of Europe are widely available on the same day, or the day after publication. The *Florentine* (*see p145*) is a bi-weekly newspaper published in English (*www.theflorentine.net*). Most large hotels in Florence have copies of *Concierge Information* which carries up-to-date information on entertainment, tours, shopping and the like. Florence also has an Italian-language listings publication called *Firenze Spettacolo* and the English-language *Events*.

Money matters

Italy participates in the single European currency, the euro. There are seven euro notes in denominations of 5, 10, 20, 50, 100, 200 and 500. Euro notes are

Language

PRONUNCIATION

Vowels: *a* as in father; *e* as in egg; *i* as in easy; *o* as in ostrich; *u* as in food.

Others: *c* or *cc* before *e* or *i* is pronounced *ch*, as in church. Otherwise *c*, *cc* and *ch* are pronounced *k*, as in cake. *G* is soft as in ginger when followed by *i* or *e*, but hard as in go before other vowels; *gl* is pronounced as *ly*, *gn* as *ny*.

The accent is nearly always on the penultimate syllable; there are a few exceptions to this rule and you will sometimes see them indicated by an accent as in *città*.

Most feminine words end in *a* (plural, *e*); masculine words end in *o* (plural, *i*). The definite article is *la* (feminine) and *il* (masculine).

GENERAL

Sì	yes	**Basta**	enough
No	no	**Aperto**	open
Grande	large/big	**Chiuso**	closed
Piccolo	small	**Biglietto**	ticket
Buono	good	**Entrata**	entrance
Cattivo	bad	**Uscita**	exit
Bene	well	**Sinistra**	left
Va bene	everything's fine	**Destra**	right
Quanto?	how much?	**Dove?**	where?
Troppo	too much	**Dov'è?**	where is?
Molto	very much	**Quando?**	when?

Some words you come across will already be familiar

NUMBERS

Uno	one
Due	two
Tre	three
Quattro	four
Cinque	five
Sei	six
Sette	seven
Otto	eight
Nove	nine
Dieci	ten
Cento	hundred

DAYS OF THE WEEK

Lunedi	Monday
Martedi	Tuesday
Mercoledi	Wednesday
Giovedi	Thursday
Venerdi	Friday
Sabato	Saturday
Domenica	Sunday

USEFUL PHRASES

Parla inglese?	Do you speak English?
Non capisco	I do not understand
Chi parla inglese?	Who speaks English (here)?
Parla lentamente	Speak slowly
Per favore	Please
Grazie	Thank you
Prego	Please (don't mention it), which is the invariable response to 'grazie' or thanks
Permesso!	Excuse me! (eg when moving through a crowd)
Mi scusi	Excuse me (apology)
Mi dispiace	I am sorry
Niente	Nothing/it does not matter
Come si chiama?	What is your name/what is this called?

FOOD AND DRINK

Aceto	vinegar
Acqua	water
Agnello	lamb
Ananas	pineapple
Anatra	duck
Arancia	orange
Asparagi	asparagus
Bicchiere	glass
Bottiglia	bottle
Burro	butter
Ceci	chickpeas
Conto	the bill
Coniglio	rabbit
Fagioli	haricot beans (*all'olio* with olive oil; *all'uccelletto* with garlic and tomatoes)
Fagiolini	green beans (usually served cold with olive oil)
Fichi	figs
Formaggio	cheese
Fragole	strawberries
Macedonia	fruit salad
Manzo	beef
Mele	apple
Olio	oil
Pane	bread
Peperoni	sweet peppers
Pera	pear
Pesca	peach
Piselli	green peas
Rognoni	kidneys
Sarde	sardines
Seppia	cuttlefish
Spinaci	spinach
Tonno	tuna
Trota	trout
Uva	grapes
Vino	wine (*rosso* red, *bianco* white, *rosa* rosé)
Vitello	veal

uniform throughout Europe, and each denomination is a different colour and size. There are eight euro coins denominated in 1, 2, 5, 10, 20, 50 cents, and 1 and 2 euros. Each coin has a common European face, with a country-specific obverse side. All notes and coins circulate freely throughout Europe.

Banks are open weekdays 8.20am–1.20pm. Some city-centre banks also open 3–4pm. None opens at weekends. Most large hotels will change traveller's cheques without difficulty. All major railway stations have an exchange kiosk (signposted *cambio*).

ATMs (automatic cash dispensers) are increasingly common. Traveller's

Stalls in Florence's bustling markets will usually accept cash only

cheques can be used to settle bills and are the safest way to carry money.

The major credit cards (Visa, Eurocard/MasterCard, American Express and Diners) are accepted in many hotels and restaurants and upmarket shops (look for a sign saying *Carta Si* – Card Yes – in the window).

Despite the high price of petrol, however, very few garages accept cards. You will also have to pay cash for your groceries if you shop in the markets or small *bottegas*. Some supermarket chains accept credit cards. Eurocheques are very widely accepted in Italy and are as good as money. Nor will you encounter any problem with cashing traveller's cheques, though for all bank transactions it is necessary to present your passport.

It is usually advantageous to use bank or credit cards when exchanging money, because the exchange calculation is done at the inter-bank rate, which is more favourable than the tourist rate. Most banks in Italy charge a small commission for changing cash, though visitors should not be charged for cashing a traveller's cheque. If you need to transfer money quickly, you can use the MoneyGram^SM Money Transfer service. For more details call Freephone *(0800) 897 198* (UK).

National holidays

All government offices and banks, most other offices, museums and all the larger shops are closed on the following days:

1 January New Year's Day
6 January Epiphany
March/April, variable Easter Monday
25 April Liberation Day
1 May Labour Day
15 August Feast of the Assumption
1 November All Saints' Day
8 December Feast of the Immaculate
   Conception
25 & 26 December Christmas

Opening hours

In general, all government-run
organisations, as well as many banks,
close for the day at 1pm, or shortly
after. Some banks in the larger towns
may open again for an hour, 3–4pm.
Museum opening times in this book
are official but may change without
notice. Shops also close at 1pm but
are open again from 3.30/4pm until
7/8pm (*see* Shopping,
pp138–41).

Organised tours

The tourist offices throughout
Tuscany will put you in touch with
individual guides who will charge
up to €320 per day. They have to
pass rigorous tests and are very good.
The following agencies specialise in
tours to the major sights of Tuscany
and beyond:

Florence
Artviva! *Via Sassetti 1.*
Tel: (055) 264 5033; www.artviva.com
CAF Tour & Travel *Via S Antonino 6r.*
Tel: (055) 210 612; www.caftours.com

Enjoy Florence
Via dei Gerani 6. Tel: (055) 051 5485;
www.enjoyflorence.com
Mercurio Tours
Via Cavour 8. Tel: (055) 213 355;
www.mercurio-italy.org

Arezzo
Futuria Global Service
Via Madame Curie 9/11. Tel: (340) 140
2679; www.futuriatoscana.com

Lucca
Turislucca
Via Ridolfi 43. Tel: (0583) 342 404;
www.turislucca.com

Pisa
Grifo Tour
Via di Lupo Parra 153, Cascina. Tel:
(050) 760 388; www.grifotour.com

Siena
Vacanze Senesi
Piazza Matteotti 30. Tel: (0577) 45900;
www.bookingsiena.it

Pharmacies

These are indicated by a green cross
sign. They concentrate on selling
pharmaceutical products. Cosmetics
and the like will be found in a
profumeria. The location of the nearest
late-night pharmacy (*farmacia*) is
indicated by a notice posted in
pharmacy windows.

   The Florence organisation
Associazione Volontari Ospedalieri
(AVO) provides interpreters, free of

charge, in case of medical emergencies (*tel: (055) 579 334*).

Places of worship

American Episcopal Church of St James All services are in English. *Via B Rucellai 9, Florence. Tel: (055) 294 417; www.dinonet.it/stjames*

Church of England *Via Maggio 16, Florence. Tel: (055) 294 764; www.stmarksitaly.com*

Christian Adventist *Via Guelfa 12, Florence. Tel: (055) 287 340.*

Evangelical Baptist *Via Borgognissanti 4, Florence. Tel: (055) 210 537.*

Evangelical Church of the Brethren *Via della Vigna Vecchia 15/17, Florence. Tel: (055) 217 236.*

Evangelical Lutheran *Lungarno Torrigiani 11, Florence. Tel: (055) 234 2775.*

The 19th-century synagogue serves Florence's Jewish community

First Church of Christian Scientists *Via Servi, Florence. Tel: (055) 211 694.*

Jewish *Via L C Farini 4, Florence. Tel: (055) 245 252; www.firenzebraica.net*

Methodist *Via de'Benci 9, Florence. Tel: (055) 288 143.*

Salvation Army *Via Aretina 91, Florence. Tel: (055) 660 445; www.esercitodellasalvezza.org*

Police

Somewhat confusingly, Italy has several different types of police force. The Carabinieri are an armed, paramilitary force operating throughout the country and directly concerned with serious crime. The Guardia di Finanza also have countrywide powers and they are mainly concerned with fraud, tax evasion and corruption. The Polizia dello Stato are responsible for policing major cities, and their police station (called a *questura*) is where you go to report theft and petty crime. The Polizia Stradale patrol the *autostrade* and main roads. The body with whom the visitor is most likely to come into contact is the Polizia Muncipale or the Vigili Urbani, who are mainly concerned with preventing parking offences and the like.

Call: **Pronto Intervento**, *tel: 112.*

Postal services

The Italian postal system is notoriously strike-ridden and inefficient. You can be reasonably certain of being home well before any postcards you send.

Avoid post offices if you possibly can – long queues and poor service are endemic. Instead, go to a tobacconist for stamps (*francobolli*). If you have to visit a post office, they are at:

Florence *Via Pellicceria 8.*
Open: Mon–Sat 8.15am–7pm.
Pisa *Piazza Vittorio Emanuele II 7–9.*
Open: 8.15am–7pm, Mon–Sat.
www.poste.it

Public transport
This is one of the few public services in Italy that is reliable; it is also relatively cheap and wide-ranging.

Long-distance coaches and buses
LAZZI *Piazza Stazione 4, Florence.*
Tel: (055) 351 061; www.lazzi.it
Piazza Stazione, Prato.
Tel: (0574) 608 235
SITA *Via di Santa Caterina da Siena 15r, Florence. Tel: (055) 284 661; www.sita-on-line.it.* For weekday information on local coaches, ring *(055) 483 651;* for Sat–Sun information, ring *(055) 211 487.*
TRA-IN *Strada Statale, Siena.*
Tel: (0577) 204 246; www.trainspa.it

Railway
Tickets must be bought before you board, and validated in the yellow machines you will see on rail platforms. If you are caught without a ticket you must pay the full fare, plus a penalty. Details of local rail services are shown in the *Thomas Cook European Rail Timetable* which is available from

Thomas Cook branches in the UK or by telephoning *00 44 1733 416477* (UK number), or buy online at *www.thomascookpublishing.com*

Eurostar Italia (ES – high-speed trains) and InterCity (IC – express trains) are the fastest, stopping only at major cities. When buying your ticket you must specify that you are taking one of these trains, as there is a supplement (*supplemento*) to be paid before boarding the train. Seat reservations are obligatory for Eurostar trains. There are also Espresso (E) and Diretto (D) trains which stop at most large stations, Interregionale (IR) which make more stops, and Regionale (R) which halt at every station.

The Trenitalia Pass is the main way for tourists to save money on rail travel. It allows for travel on all Trenitalia trains within Italy and is valid for 4–10 consecutive days or non-consecutive days within a 2-month period. A supplement must be paid for travel on Eurostar trains, or for sleeping-car bookings. Children under the age of 12 receive a 50 per cent discount on the 'basic' pass, the 'youth' pass allows a discount for travellers between the ages of 12 and 26, and the 'saver' pass is aimed at small groups between 2 and 5 people travelling together. Other last-minute offers can be found on the railway's website: *www.trenitalia.com*

Senior citizens
EU citizens who have reached 60 are entitled to free entry to state museums

and galleries and discounts to others on production of a passport as evidence of their age.

Student and youth travel

Italy makes few concessions to students. Discounted travel is available on Italian railways – details from travel agents.

Sustainable tourism

Thomas Cook is a strong advocate of ethical and fairly traded tourism and believes that the travel experience should be as good for the places visited as it is for the people who visit them. That's why we firmly support The Travel Foundation, a charity that develops solutions to help improve and protect holiday destinations, their environment, traditions and culture. To find out what you can do to make a positive difference to the places you travel to and the people who live there, please visit *www.thetravelfoundation.org.uk*

Telephones

Coin and card-operated telephones are now almost universal and reasonably efficient. The token-operated, old type of phone has almost disappeared. Booths are liberally distributed on city streets, and phones are also available in many bars. Phone cards can be bought in tobacconists and newsagents, and from machines at railway stations and post offices. Remember to tear the corner off before using it. To make a reverse charge call, dial *15* for Europe, *170* for countries outside the continent.

International codes
Ireland *00 353*
New Zealand *00 64*
UK *00 44*
USA *00 1*
Tuscany area codes

Arezzo *0575*	**Pistoia** *0573*
Florence *055*	**Prato** *0574*
Lucca *0583*	**Siena** *0577*
Pisa *050*	

When dialling the area code from abroad, leave in the first 0.

Time

Italy is 1 hour ahead of GMT in winter, 2 hours ahead in summer (EU Summer Time – late March to late October).

Tipping

Most restaurants automatically add a service charge to your bill, but you can leave a bit extra for exceptional service.

Toilets

Public toilets are few and far between; those in bars are for customers only. The private toilets are mixed gender. In public toilets 'Gentlemen' is *Signori* or *Uomini*, 'Ladies' is *Signore* or *Donne*.

Tourist information

Arezzo *Piazza della Repubblica 28. Tel: (0575) 377 678. Also Piazza Risorgimento 116. Tel: (0575) 23952; www.apt.arezzo.it*

Bagni di Lucca *Viale Umberto 1 139.*
Tel: (0583) 809 911.
Carrara *Viale XX Settembre.*
Tel: (0585) 844 136;
www.aptmassacarrara.it
Chiusi *Piazza Duomo 1.*
Tel: (0578) 227 667;
www.comune.chiusi.si.it
Fiesole *Via Portigiani*
3/5. Tel: (055) 598 720;
www.comune.fiesole.fi.it
Florence *Via Manzoni 16. Tel: (055)*
23320.
Also *Via Cavour 1r.*
Tel: (055) 290 832/3.
Piazza Stazione 4.
Tel: (055) 212 245;
www.firenzeturismo.it
Lucca *Piazza Santa Maria 35.*
Tel: (0583) 919 931; www.luccatourist.it
Montecatini *Viale G Verdi 46.*
Tel: (0572) 918 248;
www.comune.montecatini.com
Montepulciano *Piazza Don Minzoni 1.*
Tel: (0578) 757 341;
www.comune.montepulciano.si.it
Pisa *Via Silvio Pellico 6.*
Tel: (050) 929 777.
Piazza Vittorio Emanuele II 16. Tel:
(050) 42291; www.pisaturismo.it
Pistoia *Piazza del Duomo 4.*
Tel: (0573) 21622;
www.pistoia.turismo.toscana.it
Prato *Via Luigi Muzzi 28.*
Tel: (0574) 35141;
www.prato.turismo.toscana.it
San Gimignano *Piazza del Duomo 1.*
Tel: (0577) 940 008;
www.sangimignano.com

Siena *Via di Città 43. Tel: (0577) 42209.*
Piazza del Campo 56. Tel: (0577) 280
551; www.terresiena.it.
Viareggio *Viale Carducci 10.*
Tel: (0584) 962 233; www.aptversilia.it
Volterra *Via G Turazza.*
Tel: (0588) 86150; www.provolterra.it

Travellers with disabilities

Individual Italians are helpful, but little is done officially to help those with disabilities. Ramps, lifts and chairlifts are found only at mainstream tourist sights (such as the Uffizi and the Duomo in Florence). It is virtually impossible for visitors with disabilities to use the railway without help because the carriage door is much higher than the platform. RADAR (The Royal Association for Disability and Rehabilitation) publishes an annual guide called *Holidays and Travel Abroad* detailing facilities. Write to: *RADAR, 12 City Forum, 250 City Rd, London EC1V 8AF.*
Tel: (020) 7250 3222; www.radar.org.uk

The sun sets over Florence

Index

Acknowledgements

Thomas Cook Publishing wishes to thank the following photographers, libraries and associations for their assistance in the preparation of this book, and to whom the copyright in the photographs belongs.

PICTURES COLOUR LIBRARY 21, 23, 33, 67, 69, 82, 85, 94, 103, 121, 148, 153, 159, 163
PETE BENNETT 19
JULIE WOODHOUSE 57, 117
KAREN BEAULAH 46
WORLD PICTURES/PHOTOSHOT 1, 97, 149, 161, 166
BIGSTOCKPHOTO 119, 173, 182
WIKIMEDIA COMMONS 12 (AlMare), 15, 31, 45 (Andreas Praefcke), 50, 68 (JoJan), 101, 143 (Laura), 186 (Toksave)
DREAMSTIME 91a (Nicolagatti)
FLICKR 10, 108 (Sébastien Bertrand); 17 (Francesco Crippa); 24 (ho visto nina volare); 25 (Piers Canadas); 42 (echiner1); 48, 120 (David Wilmot); 51 (Chris Wee); 53 (Pat Hooper); 59 (Robert Scarth); 65 (Tim Dobbelaere); 91b (Giovanni Sighele); 142 (Alex Pearson); 145 (Pete the painter); 151 (Renzo Ferrante); 155 (Ryan-o); 184 (Véronique Debord); 189 (Eugenia and Julian)

The remaining pictures are held in the AA PHOTO LIBRARY and were taken by KEN PATERSON, with the exception of pages 32, 36, 37, 39, 40, 60, 63, 64, 90, 113, 140 and 165, which were taken by JERRY EDMANSON.

Indexer: MARIE LORIMER

For CAMBRIDGE PUBLISHING MANAGEMENT:
Project Editor: Lisa Firth
Typesetter: Trevor Double
Proofreader: Jan McCann

SEND YOUR THOUGHTS TO
BOOKS@THOMASCOOK.COM

We're committed to providing the very best up-to-date information in our travel guides and constantly strive to make them as useful as they can be. You can help us to improve future editions by letting us have your feedback. If you've made a wonderful discovery on your travels that we don't already feature, if you'd like to inform us about recent changes to anything that we do include, or if you simply want to let us know your thoughts about this guidebook and how we can make it even better – we'd love to hear from you.

Send us ideas, discoveries and recommendations today and then look out for your valuable input in the next edition of this title.

Emails to the above address, or letters to Travellers Series Editor, Thomas Cook Publishing, PO Box 227, Coningsby Road, Peterborough PE3 8SB, UK.

Please don't forget to let us know which title your feedback refers to!